IN SEARCH OF SUPERVISION

IN SEARCH OF A THERAPIST

Series Editors: Michael Jacobs and Moira Walker

IN SEARCH OF SUPERVISION

Edited by Michael Jacobs

OPEN UNIVERSITY PRESS
Buckingham • Philadelphia

Open University Press
Celtic Court
22 Ballmoor
Buckingham
MK18 1XW

and
1900 Frost Road, Suite 101
Bristol, PA 19007, USA

First Published 1996

A catalogue record of this book is available from the British Library

ISBN   0-335-19258-0   (pbk)

Library of Congress Cataloging-in-Publication Data

In search of supervision / Michael Jacobs (ed.).
    p.   cm. — (In search of a therapist)
  Includes bibliographical references.
  ISBN 0-335-19258-0 (pbk.)
    1. Psychotherapy—Study and teaching—Supervision—Case
studies. 2. Psychotherapists—Supervision of—Case studies.
I. Jacobs, Michael, 1941- . II. Series.
RC459. I52 1996
616.89'14—dc20   95-51061
                                                           CIP

Typeset by Graphicraft Typesetters Limited, Hong Kong
Printed in Great Britain by St Edmundsbury Press,
Bury St Edmunds, Suffolk

CONTENTS

THE EDITOR AND CONTRIBUTORS

Alan Cartwright is seconded by the NHS to the University of Kent at Canterbury, where he is senior lecturer in psychotherapy, and Director of the Centre for the Study of Psychotherapy, which offers training programmes ranging from a Certificate of Psychotherapy Studies to a Doctor of Psychotherapy degree.

Prue Conradi is a psychotherapist and founder member of the Norwich Centre for Personal and Professional Development. She previously trained as a nurse and midwife, worked in Papua New Guinea, and travelled extensively in South East Asia. Her therapeutic work began in 1978. She is committed to the person-centred approach, and has a long-standing interest in Jungian and depth psychology, myths, dreams and symbols.

Melanie Fennell is a consultant clinical psychologist in the Department of Clinical Psychology at the Warneford Hospital, Oxford, and Director of the Oxford Certificate in Cognitive Therapy, a one-year part-time post-qualification course. She is also a member of a research team in the Oxford University Department of Psychiatry, investigating psychological treatments for anxiety.

David Livingstone Smith is Associate Academic Dean of Regent's College School of Psychotherapy and Counselling. He was the founder and first Chair of the European Society for Communicative Psychotherapy. He has published many papers on psychoanalysis and psychotherapy and is the author of *Hidden Conversations: An Introduction to Communicative Psychoanalysis* (Routledge). He is currently engaged in research into psychoanalysis and cognitive science.

Sue Walrond-Skinner is a family therapist, and currently works for the Anglican Diocese of Southwark as Adviser in Pastoral Care and Counselling and as a priest. She now works mainly with clergy families, and is engaged in practising, teaching and undertaking research into family functioning and therapy. She is editor of *Family and Marital Psychotherapy* (Routledge), and author of *A Dictionary of Psychotherapy* (Routledge) and *Family Matters* (SPCK).

Michael Jacobs is Director of the Psychotherapy and Counselling Programme at the University of Leicester, a psychotherapist registered with the UK Council for Psychotherapy and a Fellow of the British Association for Counselling. Apart from his clinical practice, he also writes on counselling and psychotherapy, being especially known for *The Presenting Past* (Open University Press) and *Psychodynamic Counselling in Action* (Sage).

And Ruth, whose contribution actually forms the core of this book, has for obvious reasons to remain anonymous, although much of her life story is told in full in these pages.

MICHAEL JACOBS AND MOIRA WALKER

SERIES EDITORS' PREFACE

Take five clients, and for each client take five or six therapists. How will the therapists, or in one case the supervisors as well, understand and work with the following situations?

Charlie is a 40-year-old secretary to a Trades Union official, married with three children:

> I think of myself as someone who lacks self-confidence and feels she always has to apologize for herself, and I'm very insecure. The mildest row with my husband and I think he's going to leave me, and he finds that very irritating, I think. Understandably. I would. Having thought about it, I blame my mother for that. I use the word 'blame' quite consciously, because all the while I very much got the impression when I was young that she didn't love me and doesn't love me. I think of myself as unlovable.

Jitendra is a male Indian psychiatrist, separated from his Irish wife:

> One thing that . . . interests me and sometimes worries me is my early years, my childhood years. I have very few memories of anything before the age of six or five, but I am sure that they have left some legacy behind, a significant legacy, and sometimes I have deep feelings of sadness or complexity or ambivalence which are not immediately ascribable to events happening around me. And I wonder what these . . . what this augurs? I think a therapist might . . . help me in this area. The other area that I am wanting to understand is the dynamics of a large extended family . . . I would like to understand a little bit more about what affects a person's growing up in that context.

Morag is an accountant, the director of a catering business, a mother, stepmother and partner:

> I feel that James wants me to be in the house, to be there because his children are there, and the family's there. He's quite happy to go off and play rugby on Sunday but he likes me being there, being the mother-hen . . . I get quite cross, that he keeps trying to push me into the traditional role. I don't feel I've got on as far as I could have done had I been a man, because I had to work twice as hard as everybody else to get where I got . . . I feel OK always wanting to do something, but it does seem to cause quite a lot of conflict in my life. I feel, 'Is it right that I should always be wanting something new to go at, some new challenge? Should I just be accepting the way I am?'

Peta is an unemployed art teacher living in London:

> I've got a problem with men. At least that's the way that I conceptualize it for the moment. I don't know whether it's a problem with other things as well, but over the last few weeks, particularly – which is a different thing from deep background, I suppose you'd say – some issues seem to have come into my mind that are to do with the fact that I am a woman and they men . . . It's rather difficult to know where to start, except that I feel very self-conscious and rather uncomfortable about the fact that I must also tell you that I'm a feminist. And also that my father was emotionally very distant.

Ruth was abused as a young girl. She wants to hold her male therapist. What can he say or do when she says to him:

> Your reaction was – or I perceived it as being – a stand-off, and be cold to it, and not let anything happen, which obviously I understand; but I think it just highlighted that my desire . . . is not going to be matched by anyone else's. How can I communicate where I'm at, and help somebody else to understand that, and not necessarily to capitulate to me but just to be understanding?

This unique series of books takes a client's story, his or her presenting difficulties, the current situation, and some of the history from an initial session, recorded verbatim and printed in full for the reader to use. The session has in each case been presented to six different therapists. They address their questions to the client, and explain in each book how they understand the client, how they want to work with the client, what further information they requested, and in the light of what they know, how they forecast the course of therapy. The reader is presented with six possible interpretations and working methods to compare and contrast, with a final telling response from the client and the editor on each of the six therapists.

This series takes a further step forward from the comparative approaches of Rogers and others on film, or the shorter case vignettes in the *British Journal of Psychotherapy*, which have both been deservedly so popular with students and practitioners alike. All the therapists start with precisely the same information, which comes from a largely non-directed initial hour with four real clients. The reader can see in detail how each therapist takes it from there. How they share similar and contrasting insights and interpretations of the same person proves a remarkable and fascinating study of how different therapists work.

The final volume in the series goes a step further and submits one session of the editor's work with a long-term client to five different supervisors. How do they interpret the verbatim material? What questions do they want to ask the therapist? How do they advise the therapist how to proceed? In this detailed insight into the work of a therapist and supervisors from different orientations, the reader gets an in-depth view of the value of supervision.

The five volumes in the series are entitled *Charlie – An Unwanted Child?*, *Peta – A Feminist's Problems with Men*, *Morag – Myself or Mother-hen?*, *Jitendra – Lost Connections* and, finally, *In Search of Supervision*.

MICHAEL JACOBS

IN SEARCH OF A SUPERVISOR

The first four books in this series have followed different clients through a number of therapeutic approaches. This final volume uses the same format, but follows therapy from a quite different perspective. Just as it is important to ask how different therapeutic orientations might understand and work with a particular client, so it is just as valuable to ask how different therapeutic schools approach supervision. Counsellors and psychotherapists are familiar with this term, but a short explanation may be necessary for the general reader.

In the context of therapy and counselling, supervision refers to the opportunity for the counsellor or therapist to discuss her or his work with a more experienced colleague (in some schools a recognized training therapist). This is not, as in some professions, the equivalent of line management, and indeed strenuous efforts are made in many settings to separate line management and supervision, so that they are carried out by different people. Supervision should therefore provide an opportunity for a counsellor or therapist to talk about patient or client work without any anxiety that she or he will be reprimanded for not working well enough; indeed, it is often the case when starting supervision that counsellors and therapists bring the work that is not going well, because they want to learn how to tackle difficult situations, therapy which appears to have got stuck, or clients about whom they feel concern.

There is already an established norm in counselling that counsellors should continue to be supervised throughout their working life. The British Association for Counselling lays down a minimum of an hour and a half a month for supervision. Many voluntary agencies seek to provide weekly supervision, sometimes in groups, sometimes in pairs, more rarely (because supervision time is both costly and even difficult to get) individually. Psychotherapists and psychoanalysts vary in their requirements about supervision. While weekly supervision (often of one or two cases in detail over a long period of time) is laid down during training, following qualification psychotherapists may be supervised much less frequently. In analytic circles there appears to be an assumption that full qualification renders supervision less necessary, although every practitioner will from time to time seek it, especially when there is a difficult case which requires this external support and insight.

There is also increasing interest in the process of supervision, the dynamics of the supervisory relationship, with important questions which this book does not attempt to address; such as who supervision is primarily for – the patient/client, the therapist/counsellor, the agency or even the training course – and how these different agendas affect the supervisory relationship. There is great interest in what is frequently called 'parallel process', whereby it is thought that the dynamics of the therapy relationship can be replicated within the supervisory relationship. The nature of the exercise in this book may have weakened the intensity of this particular process, since I did not meet face to face with any of the supervisors, and it is less easy to catch these nuances on paper. It is interesting that parallel process receives little attention here, and the nature of the exercise may be the reason. Perhaps it is not so important to the majority of these supervisors; indeed, elsewhere I have myself, writing as a supervisor, questioned the degree of importance that is currently being given to parallel process, pointing out how important it is to consider different explanations for the dynamics of the supervisory relationship.

Although there have been other attempts than this series to demonstrate through comparison the way in which therapists from different schools might work with the same client, I know of no attempt to approach supervision in this way. I wanted to see how different supervisors, drawn from a number of distinct orientations, would work with me as the therapist, presenting a session with one of my clients. Although the project had obvious similarities to the first four projects in this series, with an initial client session, this one turned out to be even more complex, principally because it involved working not only with five supervisors, but also with my own client, whom I had seen for two years, and whom I would go on seeing for at least another two years. This dimension meant even greater care, since there was no other therapist (as we had promised if necessary to the other four clients) who could independently help work through the process. It was also a strange experience (at least for me, but not I think for all therapists – family therapists, for example) to be sharing, with the client, my innermost thoughts and feelings about the client, as they were discussed in supervision.

When I first started full-time work as a counsellor and psychotherapist, I was supervised twice weekly by a psychoanalytic psychotherapist. This went on for three years, and I was then supervised once weekly for ten years in all. Thereafter my work was supervised in the context of a weekly group (which had up to that time been running concurrently), but my opportunities to present my work there were less frequent. When the particular group of which I was a member disbanded, I continued (and still continue) to discuss my work on an occasional basis with my colleague, partner and co-editor. My case-load is relatively small, and this arrangement normally works well enough, although engaging in the project that is recorded in this book has provided me with an intensive experience of supervision, that has once again reinforced just how valuable such structured supervision can be.

Finding the client

As I explain in the next chapter, I had concerns about approaching the client whom I wanted to present in supervision. I describe there how I went about it, and the steps we went through before starting to record the actual session; indeed, I make it clear why I chose that particular session, one which presented me with a real dilemma about my therapeutic approach, as well as a session which seemed to be of considerable significance to the client.

Why this client? In the first place, while I spend a considerable time each week supervising, teaching and writing about therapy, I have only a small number of clients: my working week makes it difficult to offer a definite and unchanging day and time to more than a few. Most of the clients I see are in the context of a university counselling service, young people on the whole, whom I might see for up to two years, but no longer. There was no client in this group whom I could predict would be in therapy with me long enough to follow through this process. As the next chapter explains, and I return to in some of the answers I give to questions put by one or two of the supervisors, I do not normally take on private clients – I do not have the time to do so, particularly in offering a regular session each week. My reasons for taking on the client Ruth, who is clearly at the core of this book, are also documented later. It was because I felt we worked together well, that she showed a lively and indeed a professional interest in therapy, for herself as well as for the discipline itself, that I asked her whether she wished to participate.

I have had many moments of concern since as to how best to handle the material that has arisen from the project, but I have no doubt that the whole process has proved enriching for our work together, and for her welfare. It is unnecessary to say any more about Ruth at this point, except to assure the reader that the greatest care was taken throughout not to damage or abuse her. As a client who was abused, I obviously knew from the very beginning that there were questions as to whether I too might expose her to an abusive process. These have always been talked about openly, and although I do not pretend that consciousness of such issues is enough, I myself was able to appreciate the unconscious possibilities of damage as much as my supervisors have done; and on the conscious level (because by definition we can never know the unconscious until it chooses to emerge) this has proved a positive approach to Ruth's therapy. Like the clients in the other four books she has benefited from the accumulated wisdom of these other therapists, as hopefully she has from my own contributions to the process.

Finding supervisors

Once I was certain that Ruth was prepared to take part, I set about asking different therapists to take part in the project. I originally wanted to find distinct methods or schools of therapy, and where possible to have three men and three women supervisors. I could not in this volume represent every major school of therapy, although I knew that I wished to have a psychoanalytic, a cognitive-behavioural, a person-centred and a humanistic/integrative approach to inform my work. That some of these were completely different orientations to my own caused me no concern: I was prepared, as long as the supervisors were prepared to work with me, to take on and try out any suggestions that they made to me. I wanted to see how different these other schools really were. I already had in mind to ask David Livingstone Smith, since he had felt unable to participate in any of the original four books, given his need to work on the actual interaction with the therapist; he responded with alacrity when I suggested instead his participation in the supervision volume. His later reservations did not become clear until I received his chapter, but I am glad that they did not prevent him continuing to take part. Alan Cartwright I asked as a psychoanalytic psychotherapist, unaware at that time that he was principally informed in his work by Kohut. This discovery, again on receiving his chapter, added a dimension I had not expected, but one which I welcomed, since

I was in a far less informed way at that point 'discovering' Kohut for myself. I am grateful to different colleagues for putting me in touch with Prue Conradi and Melanie Fennell, representing respectively the person-centred and the cognitive-behavioural approaches, which I was eager to see represented. I had some problems with a fifth supervisor, as I tried to find a third woman who would give a particular slant missing in any of the other contributions. One acceptance resulted in inaction, and I was forced to start the search again. Eventually I was delighted to have my invitation accepted by Sue Walrond-Skinner, whose family therapy training was not at all represented in the whole series, and whose contribution provided me with yet another distinct dimension in my work with Ruth. That Sue is also a priest (and Ruth is a practising Christian, who knows of my own connections with the church), made for another aspect which adds to the comprehensiveness of what in the end became a set of five supervisors.

For the sixth supervisor I started with an acceptance from a therapist of the humanistic/integrative position. But although we met for a face-to-face session (unusually for this project, and not in the original terms of reference), due to various reasons he in the end failed to produce a chapter. While I regret this orientation is therefore unrepresented, I am conscious of just how much the book already contains and hope that this loss will not detract from the value of the whole project.

The process

With all the supervisors in place (even if one was later changed and one failed to deliver), Ruth and I started recording our sessions. Within two months we had agreed on a session which seemed important (in different ways) to each of us. I transcribed the session, invited Ruth to make any changes in the preliminary material that might identify her or her family members, and sent the session (and the preamble to it – in fact, Chapter 2 in its entirety) to the six original supervisors. One of the supervisors asked whether he could have a copy of the actual tape, and since (fortunately) the session itself contained no names that would easily lead to Ruth's identity being disclosed, Ruth agreed to release the tape. I then informed the other supervisors that they could also have a copy of the tape, and four of the five requested this. Another of the supervisors said that it was impossible to carry out the function without meeting me personally, which we arranged to do when he was passing through Leicester. We recorded the supervision session – as it turned out on a barely audible tape, one of the reasons that in the end prevented this supervisor making his final contribution. Not surprisingly, a second supervisor, on learning of this meeting, expressed some discontent that this had not been made an option in the first place; but while I extended a similar invitation, there was no opportunity to take this up.

Because of the time pressures when finding one of the replacement supervisors, we spoke on the 'phone for about twenty minutes, and this conversation was similarly recorded. I do not think the telephone conversation made it any easier for the fifth supervisor. These differences in gathering further information certainly did not affect the value of the contributions received from the supervisors. I gained as much from those whom I have never met, as those whom I know better, or talked with in person.

The supervisors were told in the original invitation that having read the material they would have the opportunity to ask me further questions. I waited until I had received four of the sets of questions before reading them and replying to them (on paper), sending the answers to the specific questions asked by each supervisor. The fifth supervisor, who was recruited after this part of the process was over, was the one who spoke with me on the telephone. The questions were in themselves helpful for me to address. In particular I experienced, as I observe in my comments in the final chapter, that questions asking about my feelings about Ruth enabled me to express myself more forcibly than I had yet been able to do, even in my occasional sharing of the work with Ruth through my more usual channel of supervision.

There was of course a time lapse between the session in question and the point at which I addressed the questions from the supervisors. The therapy had inevitably moved on, although some of the issues (for example, the wish for physical comfort on the part of the client) remained the same. I tried to answer the questions from the point of my position immediately following the session, although at times it was necessary to include a little updating for the supervisor. My anxiety as far as the project was concerned was to try to ensure that the supervisors, having started from the same position, were each given the information they required of me concerning the same point of the therapy. The necessity of catching the replacement supervisor up nine months later meant that I could not be sure that the information I gave was of precisely the same 'vintage'. Although I remain anxious not to see this exercise as a competitive one between supervisors, I was also concerned not to give anyone an unfair advantage in relation to the material they received from me.

The supervisors' task

In my letter inviting each supervisor to take part I outlined the method, the procedures and the timetable described above (although in the end there was more slippage in the timetable than had originally been allowed for). As in the other volumes in this series, I envisaged a common pattern to each chapter. In the event, the supervisors varied in the degree to which they wished to stay within the framework I suggested, which was as follows:

1 Start with a brief description of their own training background, and the therapeutic approach which they use.
2 Provide an initial assessment of, or reaction to, the session.
3 Record the further questions they asked me, and my answers, in so far as it was relevant to the comments they wished to make.
4 Provide more detailed comments on the session, including references where applicable to numbered paragraphs, as well as guidance for the future course of the therapy – one, two or more sessions ahead.
5 Summarize their contribution.
6 Provide a list of references and further reading.

Rather than insist on the original framework, I have retained the structure which each supervisor preferred. I have been conscious throughout the editing task that I am also the person whose work is being discussed. I have therefore respected the view of the supervisors, and confined editing to grammatical forms and other matters of format.

The final stage

If the answers to the supervisors' questions went back to them six months on, then the material which I received from them, which was their supervision of that original session, was of course more than twelve months old. The reader may well ask whether what they said could be of any value. Surely too much water had flowed under the bridge since then? Of course much had happened; in particular, Ruth's working situation had been clarified, and there were signs of her making a new life for herself. There were patches of blue sky where her sometimes intense need for me disappeared, and was replaced by a more relaxed wish to share her developing sense of self with me. But the issues returned from time to time, and her patterns of thought and of relating had a way of repeating, which was not surprising. Therapy rarely makes such fundamental changes that old ways completely disappear; most of the time we learn to live with them rather better, and, in Freud's famous phrase, therapy can only replace misery with common unhappiness.

It would be foolish not to admit that there are some artificial elements to this particular piece of supervision: it was largely through correspondence (though it works for all that) and it was spread over a long period of time (and yet again it works for all that too). Nevertheless, as in our other books in this series, this is a real client, and everything that took place was treated responsibly and with serious intent. This is more than a book which informs the reader about the processes involved in supervision; this is a record of a piece of psychotherapy, through which both the client Ruth, and myself the therapist, struggle and grow in our respective ways. Indeed, it demonstrates overall that such an experiment – as long as it is carried through with utmost care – can enhance the course of therapy. This is of course a subjective view, one that cannot be measured quantifiably. There can in this project be no control that would tell us what therapy might have been like without the intervention of the final five supervisors, or without the total, perhaps unique, process in which all these contributions were put in writing and fully shared with the client.

I do not, however, wish to 'spoil' the ending by recounting at this point the outcome of the project, except to say that whatever reservations the reader may have at some points – reservations about my own contributions to the therapy, reservations about any of the supervisors' comments on the therapy, or even reservations about the potential dangers in the project itself – I believe the resulting therapy in which Ruth and I have engaged has been more effective than any each of us had experienced before. The final chapter records in detail how I set about using the contributions from each of the supervisors, and how Ruth was herself involved in that process.

To the five supervisors who finally delivered I owe a great debt, as indeed I do to Ruth, without whom this project would (quite literally) have been impossible. They have each demonstrated a deep commitment to the task, and have furnished the reader with a unique opportunity of comparing not only their own approaches, but also the reader's own responses to the session with their own. (Following the original session, which is reported in Chapter 2, the reader will find space in Chapter 3 to record ideas, questions and feelings, with suggested questions that are similar to those I first addressed to the supervisors.) These supervisor psychotherapists have also shown a willingness to work cooperatively in a project which will do much to advance the comparative study of the many different approaches and nuances which the psychotherapy and counselling world embraces. This, as I have already said above and in the other volumes, shows how little need there is for competition, and how the different therapies can complement one another in the service of those who seek their help.

2

RUTH AND MICHAEL JACOBS

THE SESSION FOR SUPERVISION

Ruth is thirty-eight years old. She is single and lives with her parents in their home near Lincoln. Her father is retired. Her family is working class. She was given little support or encouragement as she grew up. She joined the WRAF (as it was then) when she was eighteen because, when accompanying a friend to the recruiting office, she decided to sign up herself. She trained in the Air Traffic Control branch. She has shown great aptitude, and is currently acting Warrant Officer RAF (the WRAF is now disbanded) at a flying station where the Air Traffic Control system has been converted in the last year to automatic control. When she was twenty-two, she was involved in a serious road accident, when a lorry ran into the side of her car. Because this occurred on RAF property, she was taken to hospital by ambulance accompanied by a member of the RAF medical team. Some time later he told her, with some relish, that he had seen her naked (she was unconscious at the time) in the ambulance.

In fact the accident, which was very serious, had the psychological effect of blanking out her memory of everything up to the age of eleven. For about fourteen years she had accepted this, and it was not until she started a counselling training, in which one of the exercises was to think back over her life, that she became curious about the first eleven years of her life. What happened seems to have been a combination of asking around, but also of sheer combing through her memory, until what emerged for her was the hitherto repressed memory of being raped by a group of her brother's friends when she was eight and they were about thirteen. Her brother was not, she thinks, present, although he sexually interfered with her on other occasions.

Ruth has recently recalled that following the rape she got no help at all from her parents. A woman neighbour seems to have helped at the time, but mother said nothing. When, the following day, Ruth tried to get some comfort from her mother, she was told to grow up and not be silly. In fact her memory of childhood generally is that her mother was generally unsupportive, often critical, and that she sided with her brother Stephen. Even now she seems to put Ruth second; for example, Ruth always has to move out of her bed when her brother, wife and son Jeremy come to stay, so that Jeremy can sleep in her room. She likes Jeremy a lot, and in one way does not mind this, but does resent the fact that the assumption is made that she will do this without being asked. Quite early in therapy she also mentioned how her mother had in recent years put her favourite teddy up in the attic, again without asking her, and she was reluctant to get it back down again for herself.

She passed the eleven-plus, although her father remarked that if *she* had everyone else must have done too. She was promised a dog, but this did not materialize. Father helped her with some of her homework, but he was otherwise distant. Nowadays, however, he sometimes seems quite close to Ruth, telling her about some of his own memories – he was an orphan brought up in a foster home. He shows rather more concern for her now than her mother does. In her teens Ruth went to a local church, where she found a substitute set of parents in the vicar and his wife, who were very good to her, although she also describes herself as rebelling against them. She also had boyfriends in her late teens, and although physically she was unsure about 'how far she should go', there were some with whom she felt physically close. But she also commented that she thinks of herself as having led them on, and then dropping them.

At the time of her accident she had a serious relationship with another member of the RAF, Frank. He was very caring of her, especially after the accident. She gradually turned against him, although still feeling much for him, and broke off the relationship. She now regrets this, and feels she wasted an opportunity. In fact Frank died several years ago of cancer. Interestingly after the accident, it was her brother Stephen who first visited her in hospital, and alerted her parents to their need to visit her – it is Ruth's belief that had he not done so her parents would have had difficulty coming to see her.

Ruth has confronted her brother with what happened. The relationship between them is strained, though not those between Ruth and his wife or their son. She sees Stephen as very critical of her, especially of the plans she has to leave the RAF and train more fully as a counsellor.

When Ruth started her counselling course, and started to dig into her memories, she worked on these memories alone for over a year.

She then attended a short course which I and my wife (also a psychotherapist) ran. We provided short periods of time for individual tutorials. During one of these she told me about the abuse, and asked whom she could see for help. Although I was able to give her some names, she asked whether, since it had taken a lot of courage to tell me about the abuse (the first time she had told anyone), she could come into therapy with me, despite the long journey involved each week. It felt right to offer this, because it had clearly been difficult for her to tell me, and I felt concerned for her, even though I would not normally at that time have taken anyone else on.

In the light of subsequent material and one of the issues in the session I am reporting, it is perhaps useful to say that at the end of the course my wife and I were saying good-bye to most of the students who came up to see us. It was an intense course, in which good if brief friendships were made, and although with some we shook hands, we each embraced those who obviously wanted a less formal good-bye. I was conscious when Ruth approached us that to make physical contact was only right if she indicated she wanted to, especially with the history of abuse. In fact she wanted to give each of us a hug as she went. This would normally not be worthy of any notice, were it not for the fact that for the first few months of therapy, Ruth persistently said how much she wanted me to hold her and hug her and comfort her – apparently not recalling the embrace after the course. Soon after therapy started she had to go abroad for a course in connection with her work, and she was not well. That was the first time she really felt the need for me to comfort and hold her. Her fantasies of sexual love with me were strong; and she told me about this, with considerable embarrassment on her part, when she returned. The theme of being held, of being loved, of wanting to make love, to give love, has permeated the therapy. The boundaries have been maintained on both sides without too much physical difficulty. But clearly she finds the situation at times emotionally very difficult and very frustrating, and I am on occasion made very aware of her pressure on me to embrace her; and of her anger and her disappointment with me for not giving her the physical comfort she wants. It is a theme which recurs again and again, and forms part of my request for supervision. The session I have chosen to present gathers together (I nearly wrote 'embraces') many of these issues and much of the difficulty surrounding intimacy for Ruth in her life.

The aim of therapy was initially to provide a means whereby, and a person with whom, Ruth could continue to work through her memories. She struck me then, as she does now, as brave in the way she has faced her memories; as hard-working in what she has achieved and the way she thinks about her self and her history; as pushing herself, sometimes too strongly, and getting angry with herself on account of her resistance to getting closer to other people. As therapy has progressed it has become clear that there is a further goal on Ruth's part, to engage in close relationships, both friendships with women and men, and closer physical relationships with a lover. Although fantasies have included at times a woman lover, or even a male prostitute, it is a committed heterosexual relationship that remains her supreme wish.

A subsidiary focus has been Ruth's relationship to various authority issues that have arisen, particularly in the context of her work. For the last twelve months her work situation has dominated therapy; other matters are referred to, but there has been less exploration of the past except in the allusions that I have made to the way she was treated then, and appears to be treated now by the RAF. When the change to an automatic system took place at her flying station, she was offered redundancy or re-mustering to another trade. Air traffic controllers are in one of the highest pay bands, and the trades open to her for re-mustering would involve a significant drop in salary as well as a drop in rank, so that she would no longer be an acting Warrant Officer. This, in common with others in a similar position, has put her under considerable stress, which has resulted in a flare-up of arthritic and gynaecological symptoms, and extended sick leave. She has had the added difficulty that, partly through being off sick at the change-over point between branches, her name and details literally got lost in the system. No-one paid any attention to her, no-one visited her, no-one appeared to know she existed. This may in itself have exacerbated her physical illness. She is in regular consultation with, and well looked after for her physical symptoms, by her GP and various consultants.

There has not surprisingly been considerable anger towards those in authority over her, some of which she was able to express to them in a constructive manner. Much of this has brought back, in my opinion and as I put to her, feelings associated with a childhood in which she frequently felt ignored, especially around the time of the abuse. I have continued in this period to make allusions to the past, but I also worked to try and help her deal with the present situation, which felt to me to be both farcical and deeply insulting to her, considering all she had given the RAF. But I have also linked the past neglect to the way that she feels I neglect responding to her wish for physical comfort and closeness. Our joint concern for her own inner development, and hopes for changes in her patterns of relationships, seem to have come back to the fore recently, especially since first mentioning this project to her.

Asking Ruth to take part in the project had some risks attached to it, and I hesitated before finding what felt the right moment to ask her. I did not want to abuse her by exposing her to public gaze, even though I knew that her anonymity would be protected. I did not want to appear to treat her as special, even though I recognized that what she desperately needs is someone in her life who will treat her in this special way. I did not want to presume on her 'wish to give love' to me in return for what I had given to her. I put the proposal to her very carefully, and tried to choose as neutral a time for her as I could. I made it very clear that I did not want to hurry a decision, that she could ask as much as she wanted to know about the project, and that she was free to say 'no' or 'yes' – that there was no pressure from me on her to agree to take part. I hoped that this consciously sincere message might be in contrast to the pressure put on her by the rape, although I recognize that no choice is ever completely 'free', and that once I had asked her, some pressure on my part could have been imparted or implied. Nevertheless, it is perhaps significant that she turned down two requests for help made to her by others in the week following my initial suggestion to her, on the grounds that she felt pressurized by them; and by contrast, she said, she realized she had been given a genuine choice by me. Because she was herself concerned about training for counsellors and therapists, she was ready to take part.

I suggested that we begin to record the sixty-minute sessions in September. I had my own holiday at the start of August. We met twice after my return, and on the last session in August, before Ruth herself had a week's break, I first placed the tape-recorder in the room, asking her whether she would like it to be switched on or just left there to get used to its presence. She said it was all right for it to be switched on. I checked this out with her again, repeating that it was her decision. It could just be there if she wished. I was anxious that she should be given the choice, even though there was something of a *fait accompli* already with it being there. She repeated that it was all right for the tape to be on, although as it turned out she had brought particular ideas and memories to talk about on that occasion, because she thought it would be her last chance to tell me them before the sessions were recorded. These concerned her going into hospital for a further operation for her gynaecological symptoms, and her concern on the one hand that it would be like being raped, and on the other that it would be like being gazed upon by the RAF medical orderly as he had done after her accident. In the session I linked these feelings to being recorded.

After Ruth's one-week holiday we met three times before she went into hospital for a few days. She was determined to come for her session as soon as she could after being discharged from hospital, even though the drive would be exhausting. The session which I present for supervision is the one immediately after the operation. It is perhaps significant that what happened at the end of the session occurred after the tape had run out, in the two or three minutes which the session went over the hour. But more of that later, because for the time being a verbatim account can be given.

1 *Ruth:* I don't know whether I want to be here today or not. I feel like crying straight away. [*she looks very tearful*]

  M.J.: It sounds like it might be a good idea to. You are here, but it might have been very difficult to get here.

2 *Ruth:* Yes. [*a few tears*] I feel I can't speak to you as a cold psychotherapist, a male, or whatever. At the moment I just feel alienated. [*silent for a few seconds*] Seem scared. Didn't feel like this driving down . . .

  M.J.: Can you tell me? Can you express more of the alienation? I wonder whether that would be a useful thing to do, say what it is that – what it is about it, describe how that feels.

3 *Ruth:* I don't want to talk to somebody I see as being cold, and clinical. [*little nervous laugh*] I think I want the comfort and the warmth . . . I don't want the coldness, um . . . also being a man, just at the moment, very uptight about that. [*another nervous laugh*] It would be a damn sight easier if I'd been talking to Moira or Barbara or somebody, even though I don't know them, they don't know my background, I feel it's almost easier to talk to them as a woman at the moment. [*Moira is my wife, and works in the same building where I see Ruth. Barbara is the receptionist.*] Somehow all the trust, the relationship we've built up, I just feel . . . backing off. [*she takes a tissue from the box on the low table between us*] Just out there [*i.e. in the waiting area*] – I actually managed to get here early – I've not even tried to collect my thoughts. I just felt that I was absolutely . . . tears in my eyes . . . I could justify it and put it down to the anaesthetic still, and I think it probably is, but I'm just very uptight about it.

  M.J.: Sounds like more than that, doesn't it? I mean, it sounds like that's part of it, but it sounds as though it's not just what you're feeling, as it were, in terms of the immediate effect. It's something else that's sort of around too: it's as though something's been really

stirred up. And I'm not sure whether it's something that
I've said or done, or . . . or whether it's what's been
happening to you –

4 *Ruth:*   – No. It's gone with the hospital and everything else. I
feel very vulnerable. [*she weeps a little, then is silent for a
few seconds*] I feel in one way I want to tell you what's
. . . what happened, but I don't know whether it's
appropriate. And it's the sort of thing that I would have
shared if I'd got some close soul-mate, somebody who'd
understand, yet somehow I feel, as I say, alienated here.
Um . . . [*silent for a number of seconds*] I don't know how
much it is the psychotherapy and how much it is you
as a man.

   M.J.:   What I'm struck by is how hard it is, because there
seem to be – those two factors are rather different.
You see I think there's one bit about being a
psychotherapist, and being in a sort of clinical situation
which is . . . I . . . You would need to tell me whether
this is right or not – but whether that actually is yet
again like what you felt like over the last two days or
three days, perhaps. And so on the one hand there's
that cold, clinical bit, and actually in a funny sort of
way that reminds me – the cold bit reminds me – not
the clinical bit – of you saying that you go to your
mother, and your mother doesn't respond when you're
small, and you really want her to be warm, and
comforting and cuddly, and so on. She doesn't. She says
'Go away'. So that seems to be nothing to do with
being a man, that's to do with being a clinical therapist
– as it were – bit, the cold bit, the objective bit, the
analytical bit, the bit that's tape-recording and so on,
and all that bit. So that's that bit. And then the *man*
bit, that's a very different bit, because the man bit is
not actually cold at all, that's sort of red-hot stuff,
'Don't let that get near me', because that could be very
dangerous, and make you feel very uncomfortable, and
so on. There's an enormous amount of feeling attached
to the man bit. Do you know what I mean? [*Ruth*: Mm]
So it's actually quite hard, 'cos both things are there,
and neither of them are actually at all pleasant.

5 *Ruth:*   No. I think the first part, the therapist, is right. I'm not
so sure though whether the man, at the moment, I feel
warm towards, I feel more . . . er . . . feel more vulnerable,
feel more exposed rather than wanting the warmth . . .

M.J.: No, no. I think that's what I meant. I think the man bit is – when I said 'red hot' I meant not warm, but it's dangerous [*Ruth*: Yes], it's . . . it brings up . . . actually, as though the man is not cold and clinical; that the man is really – you know – unable to be separate and distant and that makes it actually very hard.

6 *Ruth:* [*a short silence*] And yet also there's the . . . sort of what is appropriate, what is right to share. Somehow I feel that because you're a man I don't want to share that . . . as though I would have found it easier to share with a woman . . . almost as if it's sharing that's making me more vulnerable . . . or making me more exposed again. [*silence*] And then all yesterday and this morning I was thinking of calling this off: I won't come, I won't come. And a friend rang up before I came out and said, 'Are you going or not?'; and she offered me a lift down here. It was only really at that point that I said, 'Yes I'm going. I'll drive myself'. The idea of driving myself is that I'm actually freer . . . But it was very much of the last minute. I was very undecided what to do . . . [*silence*]

M.J.: It's like . . . um . . . the two major ways that you have been hurt in your life are first of all coldness, and secondly, being exposed to sexual attack; and it's like both those things are sort of come together, and I stand for both those.

7 *Ruth:* [*silent for a few seconds*] Well, I don't think you stand for them as much as the hospital does. And it's almost the aftermath of which . . . the chance to try and pick up something positive, to try and turn some of that, which you would have been the ideal one to help me with, and yet somehow I don't feel I want to expose myself to you. I think the coldness and the . . . um . . . you know, the sterility of it all, has been much more painful to me the last two days, and much more recaptured thoughts of both the assault and the last accident. I was making so many links with both of them, at different times, and I was sort of stuck in hospital, and I expressed them, and I thought 'Dammit, I wish I could have taped those links or you would have been there to hear them, because they would have explained so much'. It is my opportunity to tell, but I don't feel as though I can. [*Ruth is quite upset during this last part*]

M.J.: You don't have to tell them today . . . you can . . . you won't lose them, I think. You may want, before today's finished, to say some of them but you may find that you want to come back to it, at a point where it feels as if you're in a stronger position to do that. It's very hard that one . . . I mean, you *can* tape them. I said to you before, you can have any copy of these tapes, and . . . if you can speak. But I think it's something about, it's like you saying, 'I want to drive myself across', I think it's about *you* having the control of it, that's important. And it won't go if you don't say it today. You can come back to it if you want to another time. But you can say some of it today when it feels right. But if it doesn't feel right yet . . . [*brief silence*] What is clear is that the thing that you thought would happen *has* happened, that it really has stirred all that up.

8 *Ruth:* [*silence*] I suppose I couldn't fault them, what actually has happened the last couple of days. They were very kind. But it just has sort of really brought back all the memories. [*Ruth is a little upset, but not for more than a few seconds, but she cries a little throughout all that follows*] I knew my feelings had changed when I just couldn't sleep on Monday night, Tuesday, and er . . . the nurse coming in every half hour, to see if I was still alive, I think. But the one thing I was trying desperately, I knew I needed to sleep, I needed to go off . . . and what's normally allowed me to sleep in the past was having the fantasy of having you there. Sometime in the early hours I thought of that and absolutely went cold. I don't want anybody around. I don't . . . I didn't want you there. The thing I actually wanted was me teddy bear. [*M.J.:* The one that's in the loft?] Yes. And I actually mention it because my mother did actually 'phone, after the op and spoke to me on the 'phone for, I don't know, for about twenty minutes. I mean quite an OK call. But the silly thing was, that was the one thing I said. 'Was there anything I wanted, or when I got home was there anything I wanted?' I said, 'All that I'm going to want to do is sleep, and I could do with my teddy bear'. You know, almost as a laugh. I don't know why I said it. But that was then in my mind later on. And it was very much I wanted it to be the child comforted. [*cries*] And there was nobody there to do it. And I couldn't, in my fantasy, use a human, if you like.

M.J.: You couldn't use me, because I had become very
dangerous.

9 *Ruth:* You hadn't by then. I don't know why. But somehow I
just felt that I didn't want you there. Broadly, I didn't
want a man that I had any sexual feelings towards. But
it was quite strange, because you actually dream under
anaesthetic too, which I didn't appreciate. When I was
actually brought round I was dreaming. I just caught a
slight glimpse of it before it went; and I tried to
recapture more what it was. But I was giving a lecture,
and it must have been something on counselling or
psychodynamics or whatever, because behind me there
was you on the one side, highly disapproving, but on
the other side was Brian, my vicar, who also highly
disapproved. And I don't know what it was I was
supposed to speaking on, but at some point both of
you actually agreed that I was on, was on the right
lines, and sort of joined together. That was all I could
capture. When I was reflecting on it afterwards it was
almost as if, the two parts of me, if you like, this side,
and me here trying to use these sessions to find out just
what the hell's gone on in the past, and try and sort
me out, and work to the future, is not in battle with
my faith and my belief, and is not separate from,
although it appears to be separate geographically and
everything else. And I suppose my longing is that the
two would be integrated . . . er . . . and yet when I
thought that, the only thing that . . . the only thing that
kept coming back was that I didn't want you, what I
actually wanted was Brian around. I've never given
Brian a hug, since he actually touched me when he first
came, I've sort of kept away and he's obviously kept
away. The one person I wanted to hug was Brian,
whom I haven't seen anyway. But I thought it seemed
strange, that I was totally mixed up, and going to
somebody I wouldn't naturally have gone to, but I
actually wanted *his* comfort. [*a little laugh-cum-sigh*] But
it seemed to be a real dilemma between the two,
because of that . . .

M.J.: Though somehow, sort of by the end . . . by the
conclusion of the bit – [*Ruth interrupts, and we talk at
the same time*] By the time I'd reflected on it, it seemed
to be much more – it came together a bit. It actually
felt as though both figures, representing as it were

psychotherapy and counselling on the one hand, and faith and religion on the other, both figures approved of you, so that somehow – otherwise you were wrong for both and... for both of them to begin with – both of them approved.

10 *Ruth:* Yes. I can't capture any more what it was, what it was about.

M.J.: It also sounds from what you're saying, doesn't it, that, that – I'm not quite sure, you might want to... to... to pursue this sometime, but that symbolism is a very interesting one that you have, of on the one hand therapy, and on the other hand faith. And it felt to me that you were actually saying that in this point where you were really feeling very vulnerable and very much wanting comfort, that at that point what you wanted was faith, not therapy. There's something much more comforting about faith than therapy, just as there's something much more comforting about a teddy bear than a *sexual* man, at that point. Indeed, actually, it's more than that: it's almost as if actually the therapy or the sexual man is the... is seen as *very* dangerous and attacking; and the other side is the comforting, holding, healing.

11 *Ruth:* That's so. But neither were given me, what I wanted at the time. Actually giving it me was all very much in the mind, that wasn't what I wanted. I wanted some sort of reality. [*pauses*] Last night I thought it was going to be the same. I just could not get off to sleep. Seemed to be sort of dozing a bit, but not sleeping. I didn't know what to think about in order to try and sleep. There was almost a dulling mechan- controlling – considering the wind was howling and the rain was coming down, which – I often think, 'Oh well, at least I am lying protected within four walls instead of being out on expeditions or in a tent'; but that didn't seem to work. There was sort of no thought of wanting somebody close to me again, so in one way I want that, I want the comfort, but I don't want any – I don't want anybody close to me sexually. So it feels just a constant strain. It's easy to push people away. [*pauses for a considerable number of seconds*] You know the one thing I remember just before going into the operation is absolutely amazing. They'd taken me down and just about knocked me out... put the initial needle in, or

whatever. And the surgeon comes out – he'd already seen me upstairs, but he was all in his big gown. He spoke to me before they injected. And the anaesthetist sort of said you know, when you feel it going in my arm then I won't know anything else. And before she did that, the surgeon was on the other side of me, and he said 'Give me your hand'. And he was holding my hand – probably it was to see me go flop – but the fact that he did that, I felt it was a comfort. I mean, I was not expecting a surgeon to do that, his gloves on or whatever. And then he was just stroking my hair; got his hand on my forehead. And they injected me and I'd gone. But somehow it was that OK intimacy, and it surprised me because I didn't expect him to do that. And in one way I can try and justify it, I could see what he was doing, seeing whether I was actually out for the count or not. It was actually a very gentle move, that was appreciated.

M.J.: Yes – I don't know anything about surgical techniques, and so on. I think it sounds as if it wasn't just about whether you were out for the count. Something about actually creating the feeling that it was all right. He would look after you.

12 *Ruth:* Yeah. Well, I did feel that was OK. [*short pause*] OK, it was an intrusive procedure, and I knew what would happen then. But, even though I was expecting that – I had no idea what position I was on the operating table, or whatever – but to a certain extent, I don't know, but I would expect it to be intrusive. I am pretty certain that I must have been naked as well, because even though I had a gown on when I went in, when I came back out again it was done up differently. And during the operation I had been attached to a heart monitor. Consequently, all the sticky things were over my chest and breasts, and that really hurt me. I mean not physically. I did not know that was going to happen, so I suppose to a funny extent I expected to be covered from here to here [*neck to waist*] and the fact that I wasn't just made me feel very, very cold. [*M.J.:* Cold?] Yes, the fact that I was touched, interfered with when I wasn't expecting. One thing . . .

M.J.: That means you felt shivery? I mean, in that sense of cold. I was thinking that . . .

Ruth: . . . cold in the way of being . . . exposed and wanting to withdraw. That sort of cold.

M.J.: Yes. Yes. It wasn't as if you cut off from it, you actually had a lot of feeling.

13 *Ruth:* Yes, I had a lot of feeling when I came out and realized what had happened. It was going straight back to the accident, and obviously being brought in after the car crash and being stripped. I think it was that that really . . . made me so vulnerable. [*she cries*] Must have gone from one very comforting, trusting moment, with the surgeon to what had gone on then in the next half hour, to be made very vulnerable.

M.J.: So when you woke, and you . . . you realized that, you felt as if they . . . the trust had given way to being very exposed. Actually you felt as if the man who had appeared to be very trusting – and I guess in one way was someone you could trust, in one sense – also felt as if he had been . . . um . . . leering at you, gazing at you [*Ruth:* Somebody I didn't know] visually raping you and so on. Do you feel angry about that?

14 *Ruth:* I didn't put it down to him. I can see how it would be that, but it was all the others that were there. Um . . . I still trusted him. I suppose if anything that the being wired up to a heart monitor – it was more likely to be the anaesthetist and the others . . . er . . . I have no idea how many there are in an operating theatre, but it is almost as if it wasn't Jim who is the surgeon, it was everybody else who was there. And it was that side I think that led me straight back to the abuse, and that it wasn't one, it was more than one. It just seems to be all . . . all muddling up. I was out of control again. I didn't know what was happening. That was what was making me sort of cold . . . er . . . I don't know whether you can do anything with that. [*silent for a few seconds*] It was crackers really, because had they taken off the sort of pads, I wouldn't even have known; I mean, they had actually unplugged the heart monitor, just left me with the sticky tape. [*little laugh*] Quite easily I wouldn't even have known that. Silly, isn't it? [*sniffs*]

M.J.: [*pauses a little while*] I'm not sure whether 'silly' is the word. I think what you might be trying to express there is that . . . that in one way everything was actually very, very routine; and that no-one was doing anything other than doing a rather good job, making sure that you

were well, and all those things there; but that the way
you have experienced it, is that – and this is what
makes it complicated, so complicated for you – the way
you have experienced it, is that it has brought up all
the painfulness of both the abuse and also the accident,
and it's that is the thing that's so strong. And it's
terribly hard, because in one sense I think you're saying
you feel rather grateful to this surgeon and these . . . the
staff there. You know, you feel a sense in which they've
been looking after you. [*Ruth:* Yeah] So on one level,
that level . . . but it's all got, got fused with, *con*fused
with all those other feelings. That makes it very hard
for you. It makes it very hard for you being here,
because I think there's the bit that says, 'Well, I do
want to be here, I do want to go then'; but on the
other hand it's got all this other stuff attached to it,
which makes it feel as if it's the last place I want to be.
That's very, very confusing.

15 *Ruth:* Mm. And it's almost as if, if I don't come, or I didn't
come, what would I be doing, being on my own at
home. So you know it's almost as if my two alternatives
are either to go . . . and express what's going on here, be
in the pain of it. Or to withdraw, there's no happy
medium. It seems to be all or nothing all the time. I
can't find a nice [*a little laugh*], a nice way out.
Um . . . [*pauses for a few seconds*] I don't know. It's also
something about, it might be surgeons, but when he
came round before I went down for the op, he was
there with his dark suit, and looking very important,
and all the nurses flying around out of his way,
um . . . I think he's well liked in the various hospitals,
he's got quite a reputation. He seemed to be very . . .
very cold, that sort of idea, very efficient. Um . . . he
sort of came in and told me what he was aiming to
do, made sure I understood that, and everything else;
and shook me by the hand, which in a way is quite
cold, very efficient, polite, formal. And I think that's
why I then picked up the other, when we were in the
pre-operating theatre. I thought, 'Crikey, I wouldn't
have expected that'. Um . . . And then it reverted back
after he came up to see me, when I was coming round,
saying what they had found and what they were doing,
and everything else, what the next step would be. He
was back to the very formal, what's gone on. I don't

know, I almost tried to size it up in my mind: when I was perfectly *compos mentis* he was very formal; then I was about to go under [*laughs*], and going under he did something that was good, and I appreciated; but it was also the time when I was just about to lose my control. Then when I'm back to being OK again, he's back to the formal side. I feel there's something in that sort of change that I feel unhappy with. It's nothing to do with him, I'm sure that's just him. It's somehow in me. I feel... I think it's something to do with when somebody's actually giving me comfort, it's the same time that I'm going to be vulnerable and out of control.

M.J.: Yes. I wonder whether this sort of builds on what you've just said then. I... um... I think that, that just as you go into the operating theatre, at that particular point, you are at a very infantile state, you are completely dependent on, on these people doing the right thing, you know, in all sorts of ways. [*Ruth:* Yep – totally] Utterly dependent state. I mean it's... it's a frighteningly dependent state in one way. But because it's serving, you know, a good purpose, then you go along with it. But in that utterly dependent state, what happens is, that he... he... he actually tries to respond, in a rather motherly way. It's a very motherly gesture, isn't it, to do... to be like that? And, when you're back to where you are an adult again, what you're getting is a very formal thing. [*Ruth:* Mm] I think what you would love to be able to do is to be able to feel that it's all right to have that motherly... when you actually felt really... when you were really in control of it [*Ruth:* Yeah] from your point of view. You could actually do as you want to with it. You know, you can say 'Yes' or 'No' to it, as it were. And at that particular point, much as it was valuable, you couldn't say 'Yes' or 'No' to it. [*Ruth:* Mm] So it was nice, but it was also an intrusion, because you couldn't say 'No' to it. And you couldn't say 'No' to it because you also needed it as well. [*Ruth:* Mm] So I think it's something like that, isn't it? You would really love to be able to feel that warmth, that comforting, and as an adult. [*Ruth:* Mm. When I have got some control of it] And you've got control of it, you can say 'Yes', you can say 'No'. 'Yes', you can say, 'Yes I like that'. 'No, I don't

want that', and so on. [*pause*] And I think you might
be afraid – this is speaking not about just the last two
days but other times – I think one of the things you
might be afraid of, is that if you get into a relationship,
in which – or you *are* in relationships in which –
people begin to express something physically towards
you; I think what you're afraid of is that you will
regress to that sort of dependent state. You want to
make sure you don't lose it, that control, and at the
same time you'd like it.

16 *Ruth:* Mm. I don't know whether it's I'm afraid I will regress,
or actually fearful that I will be domineered somehow if
I lose control [*MJ:* That's right, yes], rather than me
losing it or ... or demanding more. I actually, I actually
feel scared of losing the ... or having the control taken
from me, which really is what's happened in all the
other cases. [*silent*] I think the danger is though that if
somebody did show me as an adult the affection, then I
would want to try and fill up [*little laugh*] the jars
which I lost from the years gone by, but – so I could
see how I could get demanding.

M.J.: Yes, I didn't ... I was thinking more in terms of what
you just said, rather than 'demanding' ... fear that you
would lose control of it; not just control in the sense of
'demanding': I think you've clarified it. You'd lose
control to the other person [*Ruth:* Mm], taking you over
as it were [*Ruth:* Yes], and you not being able to say
'Yes' or 'No' – that's the thing that really is very
frightening, to be in a position when you can't say 'Yes'
[*Ruth:* Mm], or 'No'.

17 *Ruth:* [*short pause*] I wonder whether ... sort of strange mix-up
of fantasy and reality, my feeling of ... pushing you
away now ... is because I don't feel a hundred per cent,
and therefore I can't take the chance. Whether it was
lying in a hospital bed, or when I first came here –
you're too dangerous [*nervous laugh*], because I'm too
physically weak just to take that on. [*pause*] And yet
somehow, I put Brian the vicar as ... as representing
faith [*laughs*], but ... er ... it was almost something
about that, that I felt that ... somehow with faith I
could trust – incredible how it all gets mixed up,
because I presume God was looking down on me the
last couple of days, but I wondered where the hell He
was at times. [*silent and then cries*] I wish He would take

me in his arms and hold me. And that's going very
much back to the child, the baby. [*long silence in which
she is upset*] Will I ever be able to have that trust again,
as a child? [*long silence again, in which she coughs once,
says 'I don't know' under her breath, and then is quiet for a
little longer*] I feel that I've told you now a lot of the
main bits that really went on, which hit me, that
although there is feeling behind it, there hasn't been as
much feeling and tears as when I thought about you
last night. It's strange the way . . . it's funny that I felt
very cold when I came here. Although I haven't been as
crying or as emotional as I felt last night. [*pause*] I
don't know whether that is right. [*another pause*] I'm
sorry that I haven't been, but I'm not too sure why.
Not too sure what it was that I wanted you to see.
Because I think you have understood what went on.

M.J.: But, I mean, you actually, although you have been
upset and um . . . um . . . there are actually a lot of
things to feel upset about, because it's really put you in
touch with things that have really, really upset you in
the past, as well . . . as well as the upset for *any* person,
as you said yourself earlier – the whole process of an
operation – the anaesthetic and everything else – puts
you in a very vulnerable position, and emotionally in a
very sort of turbulent position. But even though you
have been upset, you feel as if it hasn't been . . . you are
actually a lot more upset than you have been able to
show. [*Ruth*: Mm. I'm probably backing off even now]
Because if you were very upset that would make you
feel even more vulner – vulnerable. It's as if . . . as if
what's sort of brought up today is that trust . . . that . . .
that your trust is something which could be tried and
actually stretched; and it's really rather hard to hold it
sometimes. You know, under extreme circumstances it's
difficult to hold to that trust. Which again you can
understand why that is.

18 Ruth: Well, it's not a surprise that I haven't been able to trust
you in that way. [*silence*] When I was just sat out there
I felt I wanted to cry and cry – all welling up. [*silence*]
In one way I didn't feel as if I could contain it. Moira
was walking up and down. I thought, 'I hope she stops
walking up and down because she will see me here in
tears'. I was really trying to hold it back. And yet there
was something else that was saying that even if I came

in here I wouldn't be able to, I would still be biting
back the tears. I still wouldn't be able to let them go.
And I don't quite know what that resistance is. And I
still don't know. I said it was the psychotherapy first
of all, because I know that I'm not going to receive
comfort from you in the same way. But I also know
that you're trustworthy, you're safe . . . um . . . in holding
whatever I give. I don't know why I felt that even
having come in here I was just choking it back. [*sniffs*]
And still am. I mean, it's there but [*M.J.*: Mm], it's not
coming out. [*she is upset*]

M.J.: I don't know whether this is it at all . . . and helps, but
let's try and see. I think it's – to try and pursue this,
this thing a bit further – I think it's very hard to . . .
um . . . to see in what way . . . um . . . to be, it is to *be* at
the moment. I think you find it difficult to know how
to be at the moment. And I think you find it difficult
to know how to be, because on the one hand you feel,
I think, very angry somewhere, that there's not enough
comfort and support, and cuddling, and loving, and
hugging, in that sense, for you from me, because that's
something that when you feel vulnerable you so much
want. And why shouldn't you have it? And of course
you should have it. And I think – you know – you'd
like it from home, you would like it from friends, you'd
like it from me, you'd like it from Brian, and so on.
You'd like that. So that's the one hand. You know you
don't get that from me, so I think there's an angry bit.
OK, I may hold you in other ways, but I don't hold
you in that way. But then, on the other hand, there's
the bit that if I did, it would feel as though that was
invasive, intrusive, dangerous. What would happen?
Where would it lead, and so on? Because that's the
other side of it, which at other times you don't feel
so much. At other times you think, 'Oh, that would
be rather nice; I'd like it to lead somewhere and so
on'. But not at the moment, you don't feel that at all.
[*Ruth*: No] You actually feel as though that would be,
that would be absolutely awful. Um . . . and so that
side's no good either. And where on earth you find
that bit that lays in the middle, is almost impossible
to think, actually, that one. So I think you don't know
where you want to be in it. All you know is that *that's*
wrong, and *that's* wrong, and yet somehow they're both

what you want. You want me to both keep away and also to be close.

19 *Ruth:* Yes. It's no win at the moment. Well, I just don't know. [*pause*] I still don't feel the anger though. I'm too mixed up to feel any anger, or really get in touch with that. [*pause*] That is one of the points that came over when I realized that I'd probably been totally naked. In one way I would have wanted to have been angry at being out of control and the vulnerability and that, and yet how can you be angry at somebody who's doing their best for you and keeping you alive? Um ... I'm sure we actually touched on that a few weeks ago, on a similar sort of theme, where um ... I couldn't be angry, or get angry at receiving what I also wanted. I can't remember in what context we were thinking about it but ... I mean to a certain extent that was coming through in the childhood abuse. I wanted the closeness and comfort, but the fact that I got more than I bargained for, how could I complain? Um ... that was the, sort of the one issue that I thought of. I suppose that's been a common thread running all the way through. It's no use getting angry, this is what we were talking about – it's no use getting angry at you, or getting angry at parents, because if I get angry I just push them away. Which then doesn't help.

M.J.: Well, I think that's your fear. Your fear is that the way out of the dilemma ... there's no way out of the dilemma, that if you did get angry, or you do get angry – you *do* get angry with me at times – if you do that, that that will push me away. Or that if you say to me as you do today, 'I can't trust you', that that will lose ... you know, you'll lose all sense of any trust that has been built up. OK, that's what you're afraid of [*Ruth:* Mm] you know – that what you feel will damage me in some way, or damage the relationship we have in some way.

20 *Ruth:* Mm. Yep. [*pause*] But how on earth do I get out of this hole, because it's been going on for the last thirty-eight years? Almost as if the positive side of all this is that I'm making a hell of a lot of connections now. I don't like the connections I'm making, but we're making these things; and how the hell do I break the mould, and be able to trust, or whatever? [*pause*] Not 'care', that sounds wrong, but not be so ... defensive ... [*long

pause] There's an assault course that I take the kids on
[a youth club] and there's one part of it that I haven't
been on myself. You're actually about fifteen foot up in
the air, on a tree, there's a plank of wood that goes
out, only about three foot, and there's a gap, probably
about two foot, and then another plank, three foot,
before you get to the tree. So you can hold on to the
tree behind you, but the time when you actually have
to step you can't hold on to anything – you have to
step on to the other, and say good-bye to the tree. And
I feel very much like that. That, OK, I've got all these
links, I can hold on to what's gone on in the past, so I
can understand it, but to actually take that step, in
mid-air . . . The only time I have been on that assault
course and done it scared the living daylights out of me
– it was literally that. I had to take the plunge. It's a bit
risky to do that with life. [*little nervous laugh, followed by
a short silence*] I'm becoming increasingly disillusioned
with the side . . . with this tree and this side of the
plank. I don't want that. It's crippling. [*pause*] I wanted
a right perspective to say . . . er . . . that what Jim [the
surgeon] did in creating the trust before going into the
operating theatre . . . was right and OK, that . . . yes, I
could trust him and the other staff that were there. And
so does it matter if I happened to be physically
exposed? They were working for my good. Instead of
being very sort of creepy about it.

M.J.: [*slight pause*] You can see where you'd like to get, even
though it's rather . . . the thought of how . . . no . . . of
getting there is terrifying. The thought of letting go of
that part of . . . of going across what actually is an
empty space until you fling your arms round the tree
the other side. [*Ruth:* Mm] Which would feel very good.

21 Ruth: Yeah. I mean even that is a . . . as a symbol it rather fits
in, doesn't it, because the number of people who do go
across, they will hold on to that tree for ages before
carrying on with the assault course. Just out of relief to
have got there. And . . . I suppose that's how I feel. I
want that comfort, preferably the other tree, but I want
that comfort as well, before being able to move on.
[*pause*] I'm feeling very angry at something now. And I
think I'm angry at that gap. I'm angry at not knowing
where to move from here. How to trust. [*silent for a
while*]

M.J.: I'm not sure whether this helps or not really: but what would you say, what *do* you say to the kids that you take on that assault course, if they hesitate? [*Ruth is silent*] It may not be the same, it may not help.

22 Ruth: No. I think my reaction would change. I always used to say, 'It's only one step, you can do it', and I'd encourage them. But the last couple of times I've taken the kids down there I haven't. If they've not wanted to take the plunge: 'That's OK, come on back. Have another go next time'. And sometimes that has actually made them say [*mock spit*], 'We're going to beat her', and they do it. And at other times they climb back. [*pause*] I've always admitted since I did it once – I won't do it again – I have always admitted to them that: 'OK, I have done it once, but I don't like it either'. I'm not sure . . . so sure that's good for leadership [*laughs*] or not. But . . . er . . . I don't know why that came back to mind today. But it's very much there, the fear, that's built up. [*silent*] There are always some kids that do it without any hesitation, and I normally point them out, that they can do it, and that's OK. [*pause*] But I want to go over that gap. I don't want to go back . . . because . . . going back is . . . is for me going back into isolation, it's withdrawing, it's what I felt when I came here, it's what I felt the last couple of days. I don't want that, Michael. OK, I'm vulnerable, that seems the safest thing to do, but it's not what I really want. [*longer silence*] It isn't the time to explore it now, but . . . another thing that's been getting at me is the way that I'm . . . transferring my reaction, if you like. I mean it's one thing dealing with what went on in the hospital, but then why did I want to associate that with here? Um . . . it's er . . . got no right to interfere with here. I don't want that to be here, I know we can see the links – my feelings towards you, keep you away and all that side of it, you as a man, the coldness of psychotherapy – but it shouldn't have to impinge on it. It's not sort of keeping the hospital in a box, but . . . not letting the effects of that impinge then on here or whatever. I don't think it would have been right for me to go out last night anyway . . . but the Thursday church meeting was actually looking at the subject of sexuality . . . um . . . the lassie that actually brought me out of hospital – I did get somebody to take me and pick me

up – which was good – you know, she said she'd pick
me up last night. I . . . I don't think it would have been
right for me to go out physically, having done that, but
also the subject if anything – I don't want to know
about this side – I'm too vulnerable in a group of 150
odd people. Not that I would play the part or anything,
but it'd just be my feeling . . . and I suppose when I felt
outside here the tears welling up, the emotion welling
up, I did not want to crack open in the church. [*nervous
laugh*] But what would it have mattered? That was me,
it was being real . . . [*pause*] What would it have
mattered if I'd cried out loud? [*M.J.:* Or not] There's
a conflict about everything. [*pause*] I'm not totally
free . . .

M.J.: Yes, I think the question that you posed slightly
changes in the posing of it. One of the things you were
saying first of all is, is 'Why do I . . .', do you have to
transfer everything here? Because actually you . . . it is
of course two or three days which has been full of
transferring, hasn't it? That what's been transferred on
to hospital [*Ruth:* Yes], has been the assault on you,
and that was transferred on to the accident, and the
accident and the assault on to the hospital, then the
hospital thing gets then transferred on to here, and so
on. Now in a way, I think . . . Am I right on this? . . . I
think you do that because it's safe to do that here. I
think you weren't sure whether it was safe to do that
here, that's why you weren't sure whether you could
come today or not. I think you do, because it's safe
here . . . And I think you might have felt that it wasn't
absolutely safe to do that in the church context,
because it was for a different reason. [*Ruth:* Mm] It
wouldn't perhaps have been appropriate – would for
you, but not for that setting. [*Ruth:* Mm] So I think
there's something about transferring which seems to me
to be very . . . there's actually something rather safe –
something, something about saying that it's actually
very positive to do that. What you want to do is to get
to the stage when that transferring doesn't interfere
with life outside.

23 Ruth: Yes . . . yeah. Yes, actually, that's quite a positive way of
looking at it. [*pause*] Because if it isn't transferred in
here . . . huh! . . . you wouldn't have a job to do. [*little
laugh*] To a certain extent, although I should . . .

        although I realize that they haven't come out with . . . er
        . . . the same intensity . . .
M.J.: Yes, it's still not that safe. Safe, but not *that* safe to be
        able to really let it out. And there may be still some of
        those links that you've been very painfully working
        through and seeing; maybe some of those that you
        choose to come back to at another time. [*Ruth:* Mm]
        Even though you've obviously shared some of them.
Ruth: Mm. Possibly some of them are beginning to be here.

Ruth was just saying this when the tape ran out, and the machine
clicked off, signalling that I had run a few seconds over time. We
had to clarify the dates when Ruth would not be coming to see me,
because she had been offered the chance of convalescence in an RAF
house, and wanted to take advantage of it for two weeks. We also
altered the date of the first session after her return because of a clash
with a hospital check-up. This took a minute or two. Ruth then
asked for a copy of the tape of this session (one of the reasons why
I chose this session, because she clearly felt it to be an important
one). Having settled all this, we got up and Ruth asked if she could
give me a hug.

I was somewhat taken by surprise. In the session I had felt very
concerned for her, and very aware of all she had been through; and
I recognized immediately her need to make some sort of human
contact, especially since she had felt so distant from me during
much of the session, and was now going away for two weeks. In her
own words in the next session after that break, Ruth described that
particular moment: 'I felt I wanted to overcome that blocking-off
which I had begun to do during the session and make that stand'.
Looking back on the session, I can see that it was like wanting to
jump the short gap between the two of us, and cling on to me, like
the tree on the other side of the gap. On the other hand, I felt
concerned both for my own therapist's stance, which is one of
believing in abstinence from touch, and also for her as to what this
might mean for her. It was not my feeling either that I wanted to
hug her at that point. When I said, 'Is that going to be dangerous?',
I think that reflected what I felt about my therapist's role, as much
as her own well-being! She put her arms round me briefly, and I
placed one arm round her – the other was holding a diary. Ruth
then left.

Ruth realized how I felt. She described it in the session after her
return:

    Your reaction was the – or I perceived it as being – a stand-
    off, and be cold to it, and not let anything happen, which

obviously I understand; but I think it just highlighted my, that my desire in me was . . . is not going to be matched by anyone else's. How can I communicate where I'm at and help somebody else to understand that, and not necessarily to capitulate to me but just to be understanding?

The question of such physical contact remains a puzzling one for me, although I would normally have no doubt as to my position on this matter. I have since told Ruth that hugging clients is not my practice, and that I am not singling her out as different from any other client by refusing her wish for such comfort. She took my explanation as a rebuke. I suspect also that there is a lot more anger around that whole area, in me about my boundaries being invaded, and in Ruth about me not being caring enough; and that her feelings, and their links to her past experience, need to be voiced as therapy proceeds. In the session before the Christmas break, Ruth said that she saw that her wish to hug me was actually an invasion of my boundaries, and that she thought she was getting her own back on me as she had done (in a rather different way) with some of her past boyfriends. But then, as she went at the end of the session, she asked if she could have 'a Christmas hug'. This time I said, 'I think we'll just leave it there'.

THE READER'S
RESPONSE

3

Before reading further, the reader is given space to record a personal response to this session, and to questions similar to those which the six supervisors were asked to address.

What are your initial reactions to this session and to the therapist's contributions to it?

What is your initial assessment of the way this session went?

What further information do you want to seek on the course of therapy?

What further information do you want to seek on the client?

What comments do you want to make on the session?

How would you advise the therapist to proceed?

ALAN CARTWRIGHT

PSYCHOANALYTIC SELF PSYCHOLOGY

The supervisor

When I started to think about this exercise, I felt it was one of consultancy, not supervision. As a supervisor, I have responsibilities to both the student and patient and meet regularly with the student to discuss one or two cases, often over several years. In consultancy, it is the therapist who is directly responsible for the patient, and is seeking advice because they feel they want a new perspective on a case. I only aim to help them see the case from another angle. This is the approach I have taken to this session.

There are a number of issues to which I have not addressed myself, although there are two I wish to mention. The first is the impact of introducing a tape-recorder for a specific purpose during the course of the therapy. In my experience, it is always better to use tapes from a therapy where the tape has been an integral part of the process. When you introduce tapes for a specific purpose during the course of a therapy, they obviously influence both the patient and therapist who may have a tendency to perform for the tape. The second issue is the selection of the session itself. I am not convinced that it is useful to undertake 'analytic' work with a person who has recently had an anaesthetic. One cannot say from this session how much the experience after the operation was created by the effects of the drug, nor how far these experiences were themselves an aspect of the transference.

I have organized this chapter into sections. First, I describe my working model. Second, I consider the session from three different aspects: the therapist's style of working, his working model and his attunement to the patient. At each stage I comment on the basis of my model. Finally, I raise some general issues. I am trying to work as far as possible from the text of the session and I use quotations as illustrations. The numbers in brackets refer to the section of the text from which these quotations have been taken.

My working model

I find myself most comfortable when working from a perspective based upon psychoanalytic self psychology. Although this approach is rightly associated with the recent contributions of Heinz Kohut, his model, which places the experiencing self rather than biological drives at the centre of psychoanalytic thinking, follows a path that was first travelled by Alfred Adler and, since Kohut's death, has been developed by others (e.g. Stolorow, Bacal).

Like most psychoanalytic terms, the concept of the 'self' is used in many different ways. In this chapter, I use two senses of the meaning. First, I refer to the 'experiencing self' – that is, the person who thinks, feels and acts. I usually refer to that person by role. Second, I use the term 'self' to refer to the way the person organizes or structures their experience; I refer to the nature and qualities of their self-organization.

One form of relationship, which Kohut named the selfobject relationship, is central to the modern approach to self psychology. It is through the medium of selfobject relationships that we organize and maintain our affective responses to ourselves and others, laying down the basic structures of our selves. To illustrate, if a baby is distressed and the caregiver empathizes with that distress and is able to provide a calming experience, then the baby has the opportunity to experience moving from a state of distress to one of calm. If over the years there are regular calming experiences, then the baby will learn to calm itself when the caregiver fails. Similarly, when the infant feels pleased with itself, that good feeling can be sustained over less rewarding times if the caregiver can empathize and respond appropriately. At a more complex level, if the child is fraught with conflicting feelings and caregivers have the capacity to contain and integrate these experiences, the child is likely to develop the capacity to deal with internal conflict. The child who is exposed to such experiences is likely to develop a healthy sense of self-esteem and a capacity to tolerate conflict and distress. Kohut refers to the function of the caregiver as a selfobject function because the self requires the other person to maintain the basic structures of the self.

In this chapter, I refer to two of Kohut's three major dimensions of the self: the 'grandiose' self with its links to mirroring (affirming) selfobjects; and the 'idealizing' self with its links to security providing selfobjects. Kohut saw the grandiose self developing from healthy infantile exhibitionism to mature self-esteem, based upon realistic assessment of achievements, under the influence of empathically attuned and affirming selfobject relationships. A failure of development in this line could lead to inflated grandiosity, which functions to defend against the lack of cohesion of the underlying self. The 'idealizing' self develops through the child's capacity to 'idealize' selfobjects, which are seen to be sources of power, calm and security. Children who are able to relate to an idealizing selfobject will develop the capacity to calm themselves; and later similar experiences will form the framework in which values are developed. Failure along this dimension often leads to the experience of others as cold or persecutory. Though the influence of selfobjects is greatest at an earlier age, good selfobject experiences are essential throughout life.

Without empathic selfobject responses, the growing person can easily slide into depression, anxiety and panic. Confronted with repeated selfobject failure, they can only respond to their frustrated needs defensively. Thus the child whose selfobject needs are not fulfilled may consign such needs to the unconscious or try and fulfil them through resorting to fantasy. Then their responses to others may be marked by a propensity to shame, guilt, rage, fear and sometimes a feeling of fragmentation, in which all sense of continuity, separation and volition may be lacking. The defences the person uses against these feelings may lead to a sense of deadness or the development of symptoms which are designed to protect against the underlying anguish associated with these affects and experiences.

Selfobject relationships play a central role in the self psychological theory of therapy and change. The person with a more healthy self, one less marked by defensive structures, is likely to relate to others in a variety of different ways. They may relate to a person at one time as a 'need satisfying object' (e.g. as a source of sexual gratification); at another time, as an 'independent object' who has, empathically understood, needs of their own. At another time, the other may be experienced as a 'selfobject' who can provide affirmation, security and belonging. In most mature relationships there is movement between these different forms of relationship, with a continual sense of shift and balance. For the person with a vulnerable self, it is likely that the selfobject needs will dominate their relationships. For this person it is likely, even when the other person is apparently being treated as a 'need satisfying object', or as an 'independent object', that unconsciously they are being treated predominantly as a selfobject. In the therapeutic relationship, with its focus on the patient's needs, the selfobject qualities are likely to become dominant. In therapy, it is through the selfobject transference (in which the patient's selfobject needs and all their associated fears and defences become focused on the therapist) that the main route to psychological growth is likely to be found.

If this process is to be productive, then the therapist's stance is critical. The therapist has to adopt a stance which is marked by the capacity to provide two forms of selfobject need: the need for 'affirmation' and the need for 'security'. In the following section, I briefly outline how these may be provided.

The need for affirmation is predominantly provided by the therapist's commitment to a stance dominated by 'empathic attunement'. This refers to the therapist giving the highest priority to understanding how the patient experiences themselves and others. The empathically attuned therapist is sensitive not just to the way the patient feels, but also to the way he or she thinks, and the interrelationships between different feelings and thoughts. The accuracy and quality of the therapist's attunement is central, providing a mirror to the patient of their whole self, including thoughts and feelings which are denied. Such a picture provides the patient with a greater capacity for introspection and thus understanding of themselves and others. Perhaps, however, the most important aspect of the therapist's attunement is through the direct effect of the experience of being affirmed through the understanding of another.

In tandem the therapist must help the patient feel secure in the therapeutic situation. The patient is most likely to feel secure with a therapist who is empathically attuned to their experiences. This feeling will be enhanced if the therapist complements attunement with other qualities. These include the capacity to remain neutral, in the sense that the therapist does not get drawn into the patient's conflicts; the capacity to maintain an open-minded attitude, in which the therapist does not impose his or her views on the patient but allows room for the patient's experience to emerge; and the capacity to be committed to the patient's well-being, which often stems from the feeling that the therapist likes the patient and is confident in his or her ability to help them. Together these aspects of the therapist's stance can contribute towards the selfobject need for security.

It is within this framework that the therapist must work with the patient. Initially, that work will focus on helping the patient to adopt an introspective attitude to their experiences of themselves and with others. The therapist will help the patient to understand how they feel and how their present feelings are influenced by unconscious processes in the present and by past experiences. As the therapy itself becomes important, the focus is likely to include the patient's experience of their relationship with the therapist. While such psychodynamic insights are important, I do not feel that they are the major influence on the development of the self during psychotherapy. Such change is likely to stem from the quality of the patient's selfobject experiences. Just as the early self forms out of the interaction between the child and his or her adult selfobjects, so the adult self, in therapy, changes through similar experiences with their therapist and others.

Insight seems to function in two ways. First, it enables the patient to gain some intellectual understanding of the processes involved and thus opens the way for choice. Second, it becomes the medium through which the selfobject relationship is formed and expressed. Thus the process of 'working through' is primarily a developmental selfobject experience, which stems from the therapist's capacity to adopt a stance marked by empathic attunement and safety while pursuing insight.

In the remainder of this chapter, I shall use this model as a template to analyse the transcript of the session. I start by considering the therapist's style.

The therapist's style during the session

I examined each of the communications and the messages they contained to try and develop a description of the style of the session. I use the term 'communication' to refer to the words that are spoken by one person without interruption by the other. The session thus is seen as being made up of a series of communications. I use the term 'message' to refer to discreet groups of ideas, thoughts and feelings that are being communicated. A single communication may contain several messages and the same message may be repeated in several communications. Messages may contain unconscious meanings.

The majority of messages, from both therapist and patient, take as their subject the patient, and often, as their object, the patient's feelings and experiences. Throughout the session, the patient describes her experiences and expresses her feelings about these, often in response to the therapist's comments. What is noticeable is how little exploration of the patient's feelings actually takes place *during* the session. This, I suspect, is partly due to the therapist's style. While his most common communication takes the form of an attempt to understand the patient's feelings, these interventions often have a didactic feel about them. Further, as I shall illustrate below, a number of the therapist's messages are based on unsupported premises or provide explanations for, or interpretations of, issues which are not central to the patient's concerns at that moment. To some extent, I think this is due to the implications of the psycho-dynamic model that the therapist is using.

The therapist's working model

The first part of the session concerns the patient's resistance to talking with the therapist. The therapist works hard, using his model, to try and understand why the patient feels this way. Part of this discussion, which I consider below, is about the patient's wish for comfort, with the therapist strongly implying that therapy is not about providing comfort; although, as I shall consider later, I think there is a conflict between the therapist's presentation of abstinence and his actual behaviour with the patient. Before turning to these issues, I wish to try and illustrate some of the therapist's working assumptions.

These start to become apparent when the patient speaks of her experiences before the surgical procedure that she underwent in the days before the session. The patient describes how comforting she found the surgeon just before the procedure and her reaction when she realized that she had probably been naked in the theatre:

> Yes, I had a lot of feeling when I came out and realized what had happened. It was going straight back to the accident, and obviously being brought in after the car crash and being stripped. I think it was that that really made me so vulnerable. [*she cries*] Must have gone from one very comforting, trusting moment, with the surgeon to what had gone on then in the next half hour, to be made very vulnerable. [**13**]

The experience of being helpless in the hospital situation echoes back to the incident where she felt she had been taken advantage of in a medical situation in the past. It also evokes other memories of being abused as a child.

> I have no idea how many there are in an operating theatre, but it is almost as if, it wasn't Jim who is the surgeon, it was everybody else who was there. And it was that side I think that led me straight back to the abuse, and that it wasn't one, it was more than one. It just seems to be all . . . all muddling up. I was out of control again. I didn't know what was happening. [**14**]

Remembering the experience is very painful for the patient, who feels the situation in the hospital has awakened memories associated with past traumas. The therapist links these together. In discussing these experiences with the therapist, the patient becomes aware of her lack of trust and her wish to be able to trust people. The implications of the patient's understanding of her situation are summed up in her description of an assault course which she has visited in the past.

You're actually about fifteen foot up in the air, on a tree, there's a plank of wood that goes out, only about three foot, and there's a gap, probably about two foot, and then another plank, three foot, before you get to the tree. So you can hold on to the tree behind you, but the time when you actually have to step you can't hold on to anything – you have to step on to the other, and say goodbye to the tree. And I feel very much like that. That, OK, I've got all these links, I can hold on to what's gone on in the past, so I can understand it, but to actually take that step, in mid-air. [20]

I'm becoming increasingly disillusioned with the side . . . with this tree and this side of the plank. I don't want that. It's crippling. [*pause*] I wanted a right perspective to say . . . er . . . that what Jim [the surgeon] did in creating the trust before going into the operating theatre . . . was right and OK, that . . . yes, I could trust him and the other staff that were there. [20]

Yeah. I mean even that is a . . . as a symbol it rather fits in, doesn't it, because the number of people who do go across, they will hold on to that tree for ages before carrying on with the assault course. Just out of relief to have got there. And . . . I suppose that's how I feel. I want that comfort, preferably the other tree, but I want that comfort as well, before being able to move on. [*pause*] I'm feeling very angry at something now. And I think I'm angry at that gap. I'm angry at not knowing where to move from here. How to trust. [*silent for a while*]. [21]

Thus she has insight into why she cannot trust but feels enormous anxiety about making a leap into trusting without some emotional support. She wonders why she has to do the same in therapy: why can't she trust the therapist? She can see how her wish/need to be cared for makes her open to domination and control by others and why she thus wants to avoid relationships in which she feels so exposed. However, she is dissatisfied:

It isn't the time to explore it now, but . . . another thing that's been getting at me is the way that I'm . . . transferring my reaction, if you like. I mean it's one thing dealing with what went on in the hospital, but then why did I want to associate that with here? Um . . . it's er . . . got no right to interfere with here. I don't want that to be here, I know we can see the links – my feelings towards you, keep you away and all that side of it, you as a man, the coldness of psychotherapy – but it shouldn't have to impinge on it. It's not sort of keeping the hospital in a box, but . . . not letting the effects of that impinge then on here or whatever. [22]

The therapist explains that:

Yes, I think the question that you posed slightly changes in the posing of it. One of the things you were saying first of all is, is 'Why do I . . .', do you have to transfer everything here? Because actually you . . . it is of course two or three days which has been full of transferring, hasn't it? That what's been transferred on to hospital [*Ruth*: Yes], has been the assault on you, and that was transferred on to the accident, and the accident and the assault on to the hospital, then the hospital thing gets then transferred on to here, and so on. Now in a way, I think . . . Am I right on this? . . . I think you do that because it's safe to do that here. I think you weren't sure whether it was safe to do that here, that's why you weren't sure whether you could come today or not. I think you do, because it's safe here . . . And I think you might have felt that it wasn't absolutely safe to do that in the church context, because it was for a different reason. [22 M.J.]

Thus the therapist and the patient have a model with which they can work. It seems to be a basic psychodynamic model with displacement as its pivot. The patient's fear is understood in terms of her earlier experiences. She has inappropriately displaced feelings from these earlier traumas, first to the hospital and then on to the therapy. However, the implication is that once she has realized that she is distorting the present, she has to come to terms with the external reality and change her behaviour. Through making links she has come to understand, now she has to make a decision based on 'trust'. Her feelings of insecurity are seen as essentially infantile.

In analysing this text, I became aware that the patient repeats four messages which seem to be involved in a basic conflictual theme. These are underlying wishes: to be heard, to be comforted, to be in control and to be able to change. However, she perceives that other people will respond to her in an indifferent, often dominating and exploitative manner. This makes her feel vulnerable, alienated and want to withdraw from them. The patient states this message on several occasions at the beginning of the session and restates it in various forms throughout. She seems to imply that her most important relationships, particularly that with the therapist, are based upon an idealizing selfobject relationship in which she wants calming and safety, but expects coldness and exploitation. These messages probably indicate her desperate need to establish a good selfobject relationship with the therapist, to heal the fragmentation of her Self, which has arisen from the trauma of the operation and the effects of the anaesthetic. However, her past experiences with the therapist have led her to expect 'coldness' and she cannot expect him to 'gratify' these needs. Her response would lead me to suspect that the basic structure of her Self was not well formed during her early years and that later experiences may have undermined what structure existed.

This view leads me to a somewhat different understanding of the patient's responses. First, I would see this central set of conflicts and anxieties as likely to be an on-going preoccupation for the patient; and I would suspect that she searches for relationships that are likely to provide a basis of security (the church, for instance). However, such relationships are likely to be fraught by the patient's defensive anxieties. On the one hand, as she says herself, she is aware of her needs and how these have been exploited in the past, so she is very suspicious. On the other hand, because she is vulnerable, she will be very sensitive to any empathic failures from her selfobjects. This structure will be taken into every important situation; she is likely to experience the abuse, the accident, the operation and the therapy within this conflictual framework. If this is the case, the notion of displacement to describe her experiences in the hospital and in therapy is of only limited use. These past events are memories of situations which can be seen to symbolize the history of the interactions between her fragile Self and its failed selfobjects. Thus 'making the links' will not make much difference to the experience. The basic structures will only be changed through the experience of selfobject relationships, which allow for the development of new structures. Making a decision to trust will only help inasmuch as this would help the patient to respond to situations less defensively, and thus open the way for more rewarding experiences. Conversely, it opens the way for more damaging experiences as well. This is why the patient's imagery of the tree is so evocative – for her it is a very risky leap indeed. It is also very lonely, because the model which is being used suggests that the patient's responses, her needs for caring and security are essentially infantile, rather than needs which are essential to the development of the structure of the self, whatever the person's age.

The therapist's attunement

The therapist seems most attuned to the patient when discussing her needs to retain control. He works with her to discover what her experiences are and helps her express these. This leads to her expression of her wish to change. However, in the early part of the session when the patient is focusing on her needs to be understood and comforted, the therapist is not well attuned. In fact, he does not address directly the issue of her difficulty in talking to him or her feeling of not being understood. Additionally, when he addresses her needs for comfort, he often introduces sexual material which is not supported by the text. My suspicion is that the patient's resistance and negative transference stems not from her 'safety' as the therapist proposes in [22 M.J.] above, but from an insecurity created by this lack of attunement. In order to develop the necessary self-structures, the patient needs to develop a secure selfobject transference with the therapist. If this is to occur, then the therapist must be attuned to the patient's experiences with him. Failures of attunement need to be addressed and accepted. I shall now view the session from the perspective of the therapist's attunement to the patient's needs.

The session starts with the patient expressing her resistance to coming to see the therapist. She states that:

> I feel I can't speak to you as a cold psychotherapist, a male or whatever. At the moment I just feel alienated . . . Seem scared. [2]

The first time the patient communicates this theme, the therapist asks her to talk more about her feelings of alienation [2 M.J.] The patient essentially restates the message [3]. Rather than exploring these feelings to discover what it is that is creating this sense, the therapist attempts to change the meaning of her message away from her immediate experience of him, suggesting that:

> . . . it's not just what you're feeling, as it were . . . It's something else that that's sort of around too. [3 M.J.]

Thus in the first moments of the session, the therapist has not heard the patient and tried to guide her away from her experience. She rejects his attempt to change the meaning and repeats the message with an added rider:

> And it's the sort of thing that I would have shared if I'd got some close soul-mate, somebody who'd understand, yet somehow I feel, as I say, alienated here ... I don't know how much it is the psychotherapy and how much it is you as a man. [4]

She is at a loss to know whether the lack of understanding comes from the therapist himself or from the technique which he is using. The therapist does not respond to the obvious implication, namely the patient feels he does not understand her. He has not found out how she feels misunderstood or what the feeling of alienation is like, but he still attempts to 'explain' these experiences in terms of his displacement model. He responds to both sides of her explanation. He suggests on the one hand that this experience may be a repetition of her experiences with her rejecting mother:

> the cold bit reminds me – not the clinical bit – of you saying that you go to your mother, and your mother doesn't respond when you're small, and you really want her to be warm, and comforting and cuddly, and so on. She doesn't. She says 'Go away'. [4 M.J.]

The therapist seems to be saying that the 'clinical bit' is not really cold. It is because of the patient's displacement of experiences with her mother that makes her feel that way. With regard to the possibility that these feelings stem from himself as a person, he says:

> And then the *man* bit, that's a very different bit, because the man bit is not actually cold at all, that's sort of red-hot stuff, 'Don't let that get near me', because that could be very dangerous. [4 M.J.]

In other words, he is suggesting that the patient has misperceived her experiences either because she is displacing experiences with her mother on to the therapy, or because she is defending against the underlying feeling of danger.

The patient is expressing distress about what has happened to her and her inability to communicate with the therapist. She wonders if it is 'appropriate' to talk about her experience and wants someone who will 'understand'. It seems to me that the therapist's communications, which attempt to move the focus of attention away from the patient's experience of the therapist, as he is in the session, to the therapist as a symbolic representation that 'stands for' something else, contains an unconscious message which confirms her fears. It could appear that the patient is feeling traumatized by the therapist's lack of understanding of the way she feels. She is trying to communicate this to him, but he can only understand her messages in terms of his view, namely that what is being experienced in the session is a distortion of past relationships emerging in the present. That the patient anticipates this may suggest that this is a common dynamic in their sessions.

The therapist appears to go beyond not responding to the patient's expressed concerns. He also seems to be introducing material, in the form of suggestions which the patient is denying. The notion of warmth which she had introduced earlier in the context of comfort [3] has been given a different connotation by the therapist which she now rejects:

> . . . I feel more . . . er . . . feel more vulnerable, feel more exposed rather than wanting the warmth. [5]

To which he clarifies his meaning:

> No, no. I think that's what I meant. I think the man bit is – when I said 'red hot' I meant not warm, but it's dangerous. [5 M.J.]

If we look at the strength of the imagery we can see that most of the strong sexual imagery comes from the therapist; he has used the terms 'red hot' and 'dangerous' to convey how he thinks she is feeling. At one point, when the patient is trying to describe her experiences of vulnerability at the time of the operation, the therapist interrupts and offers his views of her experience that it:

> was someone you could trust, in one sense – also felt as if he had been . . . um . . . leering at you, gazing at you . . . [and] . . . visually raping you and so on. [13 M.J.]

Later he again suggests to the patient that:

> I think you find it difficult to know how to be at the moment. And I think you find it difficult to know how to be, because on the one hand you feel, I think, very angry somewhere, that there's not enough comfort and support, and cuddling, and loving, and hugging, in that sense, for you from me, because that's something that when you feel vulnerable you so much want. And why shouldn't you have it? And of course you should have it. And I think – you know – you'd like it from home, you would like it from friends, you'd like it from me, you'd like it from Brian, and so on. You'd like that. So that's the one hand. You know

you don't get that from me, so I think there's an angry bit.
OK, I may hold you in other ways, but I don't hold you in
that way. But then, on the other hand, there's the bit that if
I did, it would feel as though that was invasive, intrusive,
dangerous. What would happen? Where would it lead, and
so on? Because that's the other side of it, which at other
times you don't feel so much. At other times you think, 'Oh,
that would be rather nice; I'd like it to lead somewhere and
so on'. But not at the moment, you don't feel that at all.
[18 M.J.]

Thus throughout the session, the therapist is expressing fairly
evocative sexual imagery that he is 'voicing' as if it represents the
patient's denied feelings. This view seems to fit with the therapist's model. However, the most significant question is whether this
applies to the patient's experience at the time. Early in the session
when the therapist is trying to describe the reasons for the patient's
feelings that he is cold, he says:

... it's ... it brings up ... actually, as though the man is not
cold and clinical; that the man is really – you know – unable
to be separate and distant and that makes it actually very
hard. [5 M.J.]

This is a very confused message from the therapist. I suspect he
meant to say that she couldn't keep the 'dangerous man' separate
from the 'therapist man' in her mind, implying that her experience
of coldness is a defence against her dangerous hot inner feelings.
But what he actually says is that what makes it hard is that the man
(i.e. the therapist) has difficulties in being separate. Furthermore, he
adds to this message with the tone of his voice. In other words, he
seems to be saying to her that the real danger stems from his feelings not hers!

The patient responds, perhaps unconsciously, to the implications
of this message:

And yet also there's the ... sort of what is appropriate, what
is right to share. Somehow I feel that because you're a man
I don't want to share that ... as though I would have found
it easier to share with a woman ... almost as if it's sharing
that's making me more vulnerable ..., or making me more
exposed again. [*silence*] And then all yesterday and this
morning I was thinking of calling this off: I won't come, I
won't come. [6]

Throughout this opening phase of the session the therapist has
being trying to explain the patient's feeling that he is cold in terms

of her sexual attraction to him. Implicitly, he seems to be saying that she is denying the 'warmth' of her feelings towards him because such sexual feelings are dangerous to her. In fact, the patient's communications do not really seem to convey this sense at all. Later in the session, she expresses her needs very clearly:

And yet somehow, I put Brian the vicar as . . . as representing faith [*laughs*], but . . . er . . . it was almost something about that, that I felt that . . . somehow with faith I could trust – incredible how it all gets mixed up, because I presume God was looking down on me the last couple of days, but I wondered where the hell He was at times. [*silent and then cries*] I wish He would take me in his arms and hold me. And that's going very much back to the child, the baby. [*long silence in which she is upset*] Will I ever be able to have that trust again, as a child? [*long silence again, in which she coughs once, says 'I don't know' under her breath, and then is quiet for a little longer*] [17]

Thus for the patient, warmth seems to be associated with the need for a calming selfobject rather than a need satisfying sexual object.

The whole of the opening phase can be read as an attempt by the patient to try and communicate how she feels misunderstood. She wants to talk to the therapist but she feels vulnerable. He does not understand and does not accept her feelings. He tries to explain them away: they are due to displacements and repressions. Despite his statement that therapy is not about comfort, his manner and tone of voice have a distinctly 'cuddly' quality and he appears unable to tolerate being experienced as 'cold' and has to convince the patient that he is really 'warm'. In the process, he draws attention to sexual feelings which are attributed to the patient. Given that the patient is very sensitive to empathic failure and fearful of domination and sexual exploitation, it is not surprising that she feels vulnerable and wants to withdraw rather than share.

At no point does the therapist acknowledge that the 'comfort' that is required may not be sexual at all. The sexuality is implicit but nearly all comes from feelings that he attributes to the patient. My suggestion is that it is the therapist, either because of the implications of his model or from counter-transferences, who is most preoccupied with the sexual elements of their relationship. The patient's fundamental wish is for a calming, security-providing selfobject. She sees this as a dangerous wish because it is likely to be exploited and can lead her into the control of others who would take advantage of this need:

I can't remember in what context we were thinking about it
but . . . I mean to a certain extent that was coming through
in the childhood abuse. I wanted the closeness and comfort,
but the fact that I got more than I bargained for, how could
I complain? Um . . . that was the, sort of the one issue that I
thought of. I suppose that's been a common thread running
all the way through. It's no use getting angry, this is what
we were talking about – it's no use getting angry at you, or
getting angry at parents, because if I get angry I just push
them away. Which then doesn't help. [19]

The patient had earlier communicated this dilemma in terms of
her transference to the therapist. On the one hand the therapist is
the 'ideal' person, but on the other she is threatened by his 'coldness':

And it's almost the aftermath of which . . . the chance to try
and pick up something positive, to try and turn some of that,
which you would have been the ideal one to help me with,
and yet somehow I don't feel I want to expose myself to you.
I think the coldness and the . . . um . . . you know, the sterility
of it all, has been much more painful to me the last two days,
and much more recaptured thoughts of both the assault and
the last accident. I was making so many links with both of
them, at different times, and I was sort of stuck in hospital,
and I expressed them, and I thought 'Dammit, I wish I could
have taped those links or you would have been there to hear
them, because they would have explained so much'. [7]

Her response is to withdraw. During the period around the operation, the patient has tried to use an image of the therapist as a form
of comfort and been unable to do so. She has turned to a teddy bear
and even tries fantasy:

'Oh well, at least I am lying protected within four walls
instead of being out on expeditions or in a tent'; but that
didn't seem to work. There was sort of no thought of
wanting somebody close to me again, so in one way I want
that, I want the comfort, but I don't want any – I don't
want anybody close to me sexually. So it feels just a constant
strain. It's easy to push people away. [11]

Thus I am suggesting that inadvertently the therapist is repeating
the patient's past trauma in the transference relationship. When the
focus is on their relationship, the therapist appears to lack attunement, neutrality and is not open-minded. He does not attempt to
understand her deeper feelings of insecurity with him. She would

appear to accept this limitation of their relationship because she gets other things which are of value. The patient shares the therapist's views of the importance of the links, and when they are working outside the transference the therapist is clearly more attuned. In a sense, they find their way out of this dilemma by focusing on external factors. They are able to discuss her need to be in control because it does not refer to their relationship. On a number of occasions, the therapist indicates to the patient that she is in control of the session, for instance by offering her the tapes. On others, he indicates that he is committed to her well-being. However, I suspect the patient's 'acting out' by asking for a hug at the end of a session is a reflection of her discontent with the quality of the selfobject transference and her lack of safety in this aspect of the therapy.

Conclusion

As far as possible I have restricted my comments to the transcript of the session. I prefer working from transcripts because one often gets a much clearer sense of *what* is actually being said in the session. Tape-recordings can give you a sense of *how* it is said, but the listener is often distracted from the actual implications of the words. I have increasingly come to believe that it is often the implications and verbal contexts of words to which the patient and therapist are unconsciously responding. By restricting myself to the session, I can try and look at the immediate context of the words without the shared assumptions. For instance, the therapist appears to be working with the assumption of an erotic transference, but there is little evidence to support this from the session. Was there ever such evidence?

I have made my model as explicit as I could within the space available. By doing this I hope it will provide the therapist with the possibility of questioning my assumptions. So often in supervision and consultancy work the working model is not made explicit.

The therapist appears to be working with a psychodynamic model drawn largely from psychoanalytic ego psychology. The stresses and the emphases of his work appear to be around the idea of transference as displacement of affects from a past to a present situation. They also focus on an eroticized transference which would probably, eventually, be seen as a displacement from the patient's father to the therapist. Although not a major focus in this session, there is a view that aggression takes the form of anger at frustration of erotic needs. This is a model which usually stresses the notion of regression to developmental fixation points, and change following the growth of insight and working through. The model seeks the subservience of the pleasure principle to the reality principle and thus the renunciation of the patient's infantile needs and the abstinence of the therapist.

Historically, this form of the psychodynamic model evolved to try and understand the therapy of patients who were responding to their therapists as 'need satisfying objects'. Within this context, other types of patients were seen as un-analysable because they did not form the appropriate transference configurations. Although ego psychology has moved from this position, there still remains a question as to whether such a model is the most useful to apply to patients who do not form these type of transference relationships. As I have argued above, it seems to me that the patient has formed a strong selfobject transference; and that the therapist's attempts to understand this in terms of 'need gratifying' transference, tend to lead him astray and the patient to find the therapy 'sterile'. The therapist obviously may feel that his focus on the sexual aspects of the transference is justified by earlier sessions. However, in the present session, there seems to be little justification for this point of view. I suspect the whole therapy will develop further if the therapist speaks less, is more attuned to the patient and allows her statements to modify his working assumptions.

Further reading

Adler, A. (1958). *The Individual Psychology of Alfred Adler: Selected Writings*. London: George Allen and Unwin.

Bacal, H.A. and Newman, K.M. (1990). *Theories of Object Relations: Bridges to Self Psychology*. New York: Columbia University Press.

Kohut, H. (1977). *The Restoration of the Self*. New York: International Universities Press.

Kohut, H. (1984). *How Does Analysis Cure?* London: University of Chicago Press.

Luborsky, L. (1984). *Principles of Psychoanalytic Psychotherapy: A Manual for Supportive-Expressive Psychotherapy*. New York: Basic Books.

Schafer, R. (1983). *The Analytic Attitude*. London: Hogarth Press.

Stolorow, R., Brandchaft, B. and Atwood, G. (1987). *Psychoanalytic Treatment: An Intersubjective Approach*. Hillsdale, NJ: Analytic Press.

PRUE CONRADI

5

PERSON-CENTRED THERAPY

The supervisor

I am a person-centred counsellor/psychotherapist in private practice, having trained and acquired a Diploma in Person-centred Counselling from Aston University, Birmingham in 1978. I have therefore eighteen years' therapeutic experience, in which I consider my most significant learning has occurred and continues to occur. I also have ten years' experience as a supervisor. I am deeply committed to the person-centred approach, and consider it to be the most challenging and rewarding way in which to work.

While my allegiance in theory, methodology and practice is to this approach, I have gained a great deal from exposure to other orientations. During the last few years, I have developed a special interest in Jungian and depth psychology, and also in myths, dreams and symbols, and in the relationship between psychology and spirituality. I have also engaged in a period of Jungian analysis to deepen my own inner journey. Other approaches which have influenced me have been gestalt, psychodrama, psychosynthesis, transpersonal work, and the work of Eugene Gendlin on focusing. I consider there to be very significant similarities between the concept of self-actualization, utilized in the humanistic and person-centred world, and the evolutionary process described by Jung as individuation.

The person-centred approach operates out of the belief that each individual has the resources within to develop or change, and that if the therapist is able to manifest specific qualities in himself, the therapist will create a facilitative environment most conducive to growth, change and development. These qualities were named by Carl Rogers, the originator of the person-centred approach, as the 'core conditions', which are acceptance, empathy and congruence.

The relationship itself then becomes fundamental to therapy, with the therapist essentially believing in and respecting his client's own wisdom, empathizing closely with her while remaining open and available himself, expressing his own thoughts and feelings, as and when this seems appropriate. (Given that in this chapter the therapist is a man and the client a woman, I employ the male pronoun for the therapist and the female pronoun for the client.) I believe this approach is demanding in the extreme, precisely because there are no clever therapeutic techniques behind which he may hide. On the contrary, the discipline of working with the core conditions provides a therapeutic framework as a methodology of practice, which will throw him constantly moment by moment on to his own integrity and judgement.

The person-centred therapist is specifically *not* required to behave as an expert demonstrating and imposing his 'superior knowledge' or interpretative skills on to his client. He is *not* therefore one step ahead of the client, *not* taking refuge in intriguing analytical speculation or hypothesis, but acting as a companion in exploration, while at the same time allowing himself to become deeply involved, trusting his client's own moment by moment experience, and staying closely beside it. This is one of the main ways in which one can see the person-centred perspective in action, affirming and highly encouraging the notion of an internal, 'subjective locus of evaluation'. Additional key theoretical concepts in person-centred theory besides the core conditions include the self-concept, the organismic self, conditions of worth and the formative tendency. There is not enough space here for elaboration of these; however, the reader will find references for further exploration under 'Further reading'.

Supervision practice

Supervision in the person-centred approach, while primarily focusing on actual case-work, also particularly encourages the supervisee to explore any personal concerns which may be affecting the therapeutic work. This includes an exploration of any attitudes, beliefs, values or feelings which arise out of the therapy; or which may be originating in the supervisee's work or life in general, and also influencing the course of therapy.

I expect my supervisee to take responsibility for the presentation of his material. I hope to prize and respect him in the same way as I would my client. The relationship *between us* will be central as we explore issues of concern. The relationship between my supervisee as therapist and his client will be paramount. I am much more interested in the *therapeutic relationship* itself than in interpretative ideas he or we may have about the therapy. I do not in any way underestimate the value and importance of interpretation, but I am extremely wary about the way in which interpretation may be used to endorse an unequal power dynamic, or as a personal defence against the challenge of intimacy, and may not necessarily facilitate the therapeutic relationship at all.

Further amplification

In supervision I expect first to hear a reported account from my supervisee of the session in question, from the perspective of the client's experience initially, albeit through the eyes and perception of my supervisee. However, I almost invariably then ask my supervisee how he felt about the session overall, and about any key moments. In particular, I give him the opportunity to express any feelings or thoughts he may have which were for whatever reason *not* expressed during the session. I give primary value to this feeling dimension, which I believe keeps us more closely in line with the supervisee's immediate experience, and secondary value to thoughts about the session, which will almost invariably remove us somewhat from the immediacy of the experience. Clearly, reflection on the session and consideration of alternative perspectives are of great value. Indeed, the greatest value from a supervision session may come precisely out of this distance from the relationship and reflection about it. However, I do not believe new learning will arise without first looking closely at the experience itself, both for the client and for the supervisee.

There are specific areas for reflection:

1 The content of the therapy session.
2 Interventions made by the therapist, with a sometimes thorough exploration of his own attitudes, beliefs, values or feelings, both expressed and unexpressed.
3 The therapy process and the therapeutic relationship.
4 An exploration of actual 'parallel process' in the present between me as supervisor and my supervisee, as a mirror for what may be happening between him as therapist and his client.
5 Current personal dilemmas related to person-centred theory and its application, which may include observations of discrepancy between theory and practice.
6 Issues of a personal nature not actually arising out of the therapeutic relationship itself, but affecting and possibly influencing it.

I see my role as supervisor to be one of offering support, and challenge, while following broadly the areas mentioned above and also contributing occasionally a different perspective, where this feels appropriate.

I need to make two comments on my individual style and on the issue of Interpretation.

1 My own style, both as a psychotherapist and as a supervisor, does I believe include considerable flexibility, dependent entirely on what I feel is called forth or drawn from me by each individual client or supervisee. While my own theoretical orientation derives essentially as I have stated above, from the person-centred approach and from Carl Jung, my response here to Michael and Ruth draws almost entirely from the former.

2 While some person-centred therapists may be highly circumspect with respect to the use of interpretation, interpretative responses do feature in my practice, although I hope I am careful about judging the appropriateness of such responses. I always try to take the lead from my client. When she is clearly grappling with understanding in this way, I too might participate in an interpretative dialogue. However, I share the views of Carl Rogers, who asserts that an interpretation *which is not experienced by the client as meaningful and true* cannot be correct. He also casts doubt on the ultimate usefulness of interpretation: 'In order for behaviour to change, a change in perception must be *experienced*. Intellectual knowledge cannot substitute for this' (Rogers 1951: 222).

Initial assessment

When I first read the transcript, I had numerous reactions and responses. First, I would sincerely like to commend Michael on undertaking this project. It seems to me to take very considerable courage to risk exposing one's practice in this way. It is often easy even in supervision to conceal the actual content of one's practice by talking *about* it, whereas working with tapes or transcripts, thereby exposing the *actual* work, is infinitely more revealing, and therefore must induce a higher degree of vulnerability in the supervisee. However, on my first reading, many of the doubts I had about accepting the invitation to write this chapter were confirmed.

The first was how to proceed at all! How on earth can a person-centred practitioner who in supervision as in therapy focuses so predominantly on *the relationship created with the supervisee*, possibly supervise a transcript! Having once agreed to take part, I realized increasingly that this posed a greater and greater difficulty for me. I resolved that the only way I could proceed was to declare my dilemmas, to stay true to my own integrity, and to consider that I might have to write very hypothetically, since my responses as a supervisor would be ordinarily determined by the process taking place in my supervisee. However, I understood the very purpose and value of compiling this book was to try and discover how some theoretical differences might be represented in supervision practice, so perhaps my own initial discomfort with participating in this written exercise would become 'par for the course'.

My second doubt was about the differences between our two theoretical approaches, resulting in significant differences in practice. There are such fundamental theoretical differences between person-centred and psychodynamic approaches, which immediately make themselves felt in practice, that this project seemed to me to become acutely unreal in two ways. First, I doubt whether I would in practice ever agree to engage in a supervision contract with a psychodynamic practitioner at all! Second, I realized that in responding to Michael's material, I would have to free myself to be much more challenging than I would be with a supervisee with whom I shared beliefs and basic assumptions arising out of person-centred theory and practice. This challenging ambience would give a rather distorted impression of my usual supervision practice, in which I believe any challenge I offer is modified by a great deal more support, acceptance and understanding than I am apparently offering here!

Thirdly I was quite astonished by the length of many of Michael's responses. While occasionally I would consider a lengthy response appropriate, here it seems that Michael's responses had become consistently lengthy, sometimes equal in length even to Ruth's, or occasionally even longer. Similarly, I found many of Ruth's statements very long. Although I would expect Ruth to say a great deal more than Michael, I believe I would interject more often. This could help towards reducing the number of issues arising from any one of her statements. It seems extremely difficult at the moment for the therapist to respond accurately due to an overload of content.

Then there was the issue of coldness and interpretation versus empathy and congruence. There seems to be a repeated theme in the session, of Ruth's experience of 'the coldness of psychotherapy'. I was most curious about whether this experience of coldness was actually arising *out of the nature of the relationship* between Ruth and Michael. While I acknowledge that some of the themes in Ruth's life may have given rise to experiences of 'coldness' in her past, I found many of Michael's responses extremely intellectual in nature, and also highly interpretative, often introducing rather loaded words or ideas that Ruth had not even used herself, like 'dangerous'. I missed at times a sense of him 'tracking her', which genuine empathy can create. Accurate and disciplined empathy can greatly enhance the sense of the client's feeling in 'control', as it can also enhance her experience of her therapist's *warmth*. Too much interpretation may, I believe, contribute significantly towards the client's experience of coldness and of lack of control.

My fifth concern was about touch and transference. I was puzzled and intrigued by Michael's own position on these issues, which I imagined to be clear and unequivocal, more especially on touch than on transference, to which I return below. Where I felt myself to have some considerable flexibility about these themes, I sensed that Michael's unequivocal stand might actually be placing him in a theoretical straitjacket. I became increasingly curious about any feelings he had which were *not* being expressed.

I also had some concern about the choice of client, and I was somewhat surprised that for this exercise Michael had chosen a client who had suffered sexual abuse. I felt some concern and protectiveness towards her, hoping that she really did feel fine about participating in this exercise, and that she had not just agreed to this to please Michael.

The last of the main issues for me was mutuality and intimacy. While this session seems to contain a high degree of implied intimacy in the relationship between Ruth and Michael, I felt I was missing what I would call Michael's expressed congruence. This gave me the impression of a lack of mutuality, with Ruth having to do more than her fair share of the emotional work. This missing element leads me later in this chapter to comment on my sense of Michael's self-restraint.

Further information requested

I was impressed by Michael's willingness to reply so openly and honestly to my questions, some of which are quite probing. In this section, I do not include his whole response to any one question; instead, I quote the sentences which seem most pertinent.

1 *Can you tell me more about the* context *in which you have been working with Ruth? Is this a private practice in your own home, or are you working within an agency? If it is at home, is the room separated from your living environment?*
I see her at the end of my morning I give to the University

Counselling Service ... She is a client whom I see privately, indeed the only client I see privately ...

2 *What was the frequency of sessions, and has this remained the same throughout therapy? Have you been working in the context of any contract with reviews, or do I take it that the sessions are open-ended?*
Once a week. It has always been once a week ... We have never put reviews in as a matter of course, i.e. not planned; but Ruth does check out her progress from time to time ... You are right to assume the contract is an open-ended one ...

3 *I assume she is paying you. I would like to know how much, and whether money has been an issue at all.*
She pays me £22 a session – a full hour, because she comes a long way and has travel costs on top ... I normally see clients for 45 minutes. So I see her for less than I usually charge per hour ...

4 *Is Ruth still in therapy with you now? If so, how is the relationship between you now?*
Yes, she is still in therapy ... I have a sense we will be continuing to meet for another year, but perhaps not much longer than that ...

5 *During the course of therapy, has the issue of leaving home arisen at all?*
No.

6 *Some of your responses seem to me quite lengthy. Is this your normal style to sometimes respond at considerable length, or is this special to your relationship with Ruth?*
You are quite right to pick this up. That is a very helpful observation, and I am glad you have raised it ... The interventions I make in the session are longer than I think I usually make, and rather more frequent ... though what would happen if I typed out other sessions? Also reading the transcript through made me realize that I can repeat myself two or three times even when responding to a client – a trait which comes from my teaching ... I think this was a session in which I felt an increasing sense of contact.

7 *When you agreed together to record the sessions, was Ruth told that at any moment she could switch off the tape-recorder, or did the choice/control issue pertain to recording versus not recording?*

Only the latter . . . I certainly did not think of telling her she could switch it off if necessary during the session. That's an interesting point . . . We no longer record the sessions, by the way.

8 *Were you in any way surprised that Ruth wanted to come for this session so close to her discharge from hospital? (I am assuming her discharge was the day before.)*
Her discharge was indeed the day before. I should say that since Christmas 1993 she has been wanting to test out her capacity to be less dependent, as she sees it, on me.

9 *Although you have in your transcript said a little about your own experiencing during this session, especially at the very end, I have some further questions which are crucial to my own way of working. These refer not to what occurred as is recorded in the transcript and tape, but they refer to your own feelings, and any particular moment of difficulty/problem for you, which I would hope we could explore together in the context of a supervision session. Although you have touched on this I ask you please to amplify.*
There is much that I like about her. I like her courage in working on these issues when she has had such a hard deal, and suffered from long-term repression of memories . . . My main negative feelings are irritation, sometimes more intense anger, when she pushes at me to give her more, especially in the way of hugging (I have to say that is one of the words that grates!) . . . Also frustration at the conditions I have put myself into – an hour's session rather than 45 minutes (because of her travelling this distance), together with some anxiety as to whether she will ever leave!

. . . I am most conscious of my *working* with her rather than *feeling* a lot . . . I am also aware as I get into this question that there is a lot more of this type of feeling in me than I was aware of before you asked me the question. It tends to get submerged beneath the wish to work well . . . My problem with her is now one of how to help her to find satisfaction in her life in terms of close personal relationships, such as would enable her both to leave therapy, and to have greater opportunities for closeness than therapy can provide her with . . . I feel we have come a fair way now, but am aware that the image of the plank between the two trees in the session I sent you remains as true as it ever was. It is not a huge problem, but it is the cause of the greatest point of pressure in the therapy as I experience it now. And this clearly bears some resemblance to the more physical pressure for a hug I experienced in the session I reported to you.

10 *You mention at the end of the text, 'I suspect also that there is a lot more anger around that whole area, in me about my boundaries being invaded'. I would like to know or understand a great deal more about this anger, and what this statement means for you.*

It arises mostly from the feeling that I have given her a huge amount and yet it is not enough. I don't want to exaggerate this, because Ruth is actually not demanding in an overt way, and she has needed permission to express her demands.

She would I guess normally tend to hold herself back. It is therefore in some ways a breakthrough that she can express that need and put that pressure on me, and it is my responsibility as a therapist to contain and weather that. My anger likewise is one which I have to allow myself to get in touch with. I think I do not betray it to her in the way I relate to her in the session – if anything, I suspect I compensate for it by becoming more giving than some therapists would be . . .

But I am aware sometimes, when the pressure from her is at its height, to speak more, to give her solutions, hug her or whatever, that in me there is a voice which says: 'Bloody hell – I give you an hour, not 45 minutes, I see you for £22 not £25, I see you as a private client when I don't see anyone else in that way'. And I guess such feelings do influence the way I am as a therapist, although I can only see the compensatory mechanism in me, reacting against such feelings by continuing to be generous.

11 *What do you feel are the particular questions/dilemmas/problems/difficulties you would bring to the supervision session?*

It is partly about the question of touch, or as Ruth puts it, 'I want a hug' – a phrase which grates on me. But I suppose it is also about how to be empathic and yet at the same time not do anything which could be experienced as abusive. I am aware that it is very difficult ever to be right on that one: too much for some abused people is abusive, too little for others is abusive. So that is a big dilemma in the session, given her both wanting to keep me at a distance and yet wanting to be near to me all in the course of the same session.

12 *In reading the transcript, do you feel particularly troubled by any one of your own responses?*
I am troubled by them being too long in many instances, by the nonsensical way I speak – although I notice this is a feature of much speech when it is recorded and transcribed – and the fact it is all in print for everyone to read how incoherent I am. [Michael referred to actual examples from the transcribed numbered paragraphs, to which I return in the next section.]

13 *I am under the impression that there may be two areas in particular in which the differences in our own theoretical models may have significant consequences in practice: transference and touch. Could you describe your beliefs around transference, and whether or not you would consider it necessary for the transference to be made and worked with in order for progress to be made?*
I think the therapeutic relationship is an extraordinarily complex one, and transference is only one of five elements in it . . . I am these days not sure how useful the word transference is, except as a way of trying to understand some exaggerated reactions or feelings people have to others, including their therapist. It seems to me that transference does occur in every relationship, and that finding what is real in the other is an impossible task. We are all highly subjective, in the way we react to and perceive others. In therapy itself, I would scarcely ever use the word transference, although in the session you have I use the word transferring quite a lot (towards the end of [22 M.J.]), although you will notice that I am picking up Ruth's own phrase, 'transferring my reaction' . . . I work with what people experience and feel, and I sometimes make links, when they are clear, to the way they feel or have felt towards others present and past. This often helps us to understand the *total experience* . . . I never use transference to explain away such reactions and feelings in the present, which is something I fear some psychoanalytic therapists appear to do.

14 *In the final paragraph of Chapter 2 with respect to the issue of touch, you say, 'I would normally have no doubt as to my position on this matter'. I understand therefore that you do have a very clear position on this. Can you tell me precisely what it is? Also, I deduce from this that on this occasion you doubted that position. What were your doubts?*
I would normally have no doubt at all that I would not

touch a client in the course of therapy – occasionally, I might shake hands with a client who insists on it, or touch an arm as they leave. I have not been averse to embracing a client at the end of the last session. Indeed, I wish that I could feel that I could do this with Ruth in a way that was not artificial (as I experience my response to her wish for a hug from me would be if I fell in with it), but would be genuine and spontaneous. But otherwise it is 'no touch', certainly no comforting by an arm round a shoulder or holding a hand. I am very firm on that, and I have hardly had more than one occasion when a client has complained about this stance.

My doubts on this occasion were that Ruth was clearly deeply wounded by the experience of being in hospital. She had in a sense come to me for comfort. I felt that the operation had been sexually invasive in the way her history of being abused was. Therefore, I did not want to abuse her. But neither did I want to leave her comfortless, and abuse her by neglect.

Although I am fairly sure of my own boundaries, as a matter of principle I admire the work and writing of Peter Lomas, and he certainly suggests that touch or comfort is not wrong. So one of my role models suggests something is OK when I am generally not sure about it. So I then wonder is it me being awkward and difficult, and therefore neglecting Ruth? Or is it that Ruth is putting me into the position of being the one who is seen as neglecting her, when actually I have on most things far from neglected her?

It is as if Ruth is pushing at the very place where in this therapy at least I find myself questioning what is right. I think I know my position, and I think normally I would feel OK about it. But it is Ruth's persistence that makes me doubt. Is that her finding a weak spot, or is it me being depriving? In the end, of course, when in doubt don't. But that does not absolve me of the feeling that I am being hard on her.

Detailed comments on the session

In every respect in which we make an object of the person – whether by diagnosing him, analysing, or perceiving him impersonally in a case history – we stand in the way of our therapeutic goal. To make an object of a person has been helpful in treating physical ills; it has not been successful in treating psychological ills. We are deeply helpful only when we relate as persons, when we risk ourselves as persons in the relationship, when we experience the other as a person in his own right. Only then is there a meeting at a depth that dissolves the pain of aloneness in both client and therapist.

(Rogers 1980: 179)

This was written by Carl Rogers at the end of a chapter in which he tells the story of a young woman named Ellen West who out of love for her parents, and her father in particular, surrendered her own capacity for trusting her own experience. She substituted theirs, broke off her engagement from the man she loved and was engaged to, became increasingly alienated from herself, and was subsequently treated by doctors as an object, which thereby *confirmed* this alienation, rather than reversing it. She was then written off as a 'hopeless case'. She subsequently committed suicide.

I tell this story here by way of illustrating my own therapeutic and supervisory stance, in which I believe fundamentally that the experience and feelings of the client are to be deeply and consistently trusted, if therapy is to be effective and healing. In practice there is, I believe, a great deal of difference between the therapist who helps his client to *see* feelings, and the therapist who enables his client to *experience* feelings. The first can result in an over-focus on analysis, an apparent understanding and an introjection of the therapist's meanings, thereby reinforcing the alienation from self which the above example illustrates. The second will enable his client to enter more fully into his own immediate experience, thereby affirming his own value, trust and confidence in herself.

I also believe that therapy is essentially about healing, the healing of wounds, and that this healing will only take place if the therapist is willing to take the risk of meeting, which Martin Buber (1958) calls the 'I–Thou' relationship. When this willingness for meeting is present, this very possibility for meeting creates the quality of relationship in which healing may occur.

In this written supervision of one session, I shall question what exactly Ruth and Michael are both saying and experiencing at any given moment and overall. I am looking not only for Michael's ability to come alongside Ruth as she shares her world (the exercise of acceptance and empathy), but also for Michael's ability to use himself, and to share himself when appropriate (the expression of congruence). As a therapist, *acceptance* involves the unconditional prizing and respect for my client; *empathy* involves the disciplined attending moment by moment to my client's subjective reality, listening to her and communicating as accurately as possible something of the content and feelings which I am hearing her share with me; and *congruence* involves both the ability to be close to all that is going on within myself, together with the willingness for this experience to be present in my communication with my client.

With these themes in mind, I consider the transcript. The quotations are partial, key sentences, which I have extracted as they seem to me to contain essential themes.

My initial response to Ruth and to Michael when I read the transcript is to discover I feel most engaged with Ruth towards the end of the session [sections **18–22**], beginning with some of the following comment:

> . . . and how the hell do I break the mould, and be able to trust, or whatever? [**20**]

I feel we are now with the central theme for Ruth; I find myself deeply engaged at this moment, wanting to reach out, to support and encourage her in her wish to move forwards. Theoretically, I understand this statement as her wish to change her self-concept, from one of lack of trust in herself and others, to a new state in which she could feel real confidence, and could dare to trust. I then love her image of the trees and the plank of wood as a metaphor for the psychic challenge she now faces. She goes on to associate her desire to trust herself with her desire to also trust other people:

> I'm becoming increasingly disillusioned with the side . . . with this tree and this side of the plank. I don't want that. It's crippling. [*pause*] I wanted a right perspective to say . . . er . . . that what Jim [the surgeon] did in creating the trust before going into the operating theatre . . . was right and OK, that . . . yes, I could trust him and the other staff that were there. [**20**]

I very much like Michael's next response, which feels to me at last to be very pertinent, simpler, shorter:

> You can see where you'd like to get, even though it's rather . . . the thought of how . . . no . . . of getting there is terrifying. [**20** M.J.]

This response somehow stays with the poignancy of Ruth's previous statement, and encourages the struggling emergence of her new self. A few moments later, however, she says:

> And . . . I suppose that's how I feel. I want that comfort, preferably the other tree, but I want that comfort as well, before being able to move on. [*pause*] I'm feeling very angry at something now. And I think I'm angry at that gap. I'm

angry at not knowing where to move from here. How to trust. [21]

It then seems to me that Michael misses [21 M.J.] this crucial opportunity to reflect and affirm her anger, and stay closely beside her in the present. Instead, I experience his response as a sidestep, which moves her away from her own direct experiencing of herself. He asks her what advice she would give to the kids on the assault course, if they hesitated. Where, I wonder, is he placing himself existentially at this crucial moment in the session, when it seems to me Ruth most needs him to be fully present for her, to enable her to engage with *her present feelings*, as a prerequisite to moving out of her conflicted state? At this moment I feel he is most absent. Ruth then says:

> I want to go over that gap. I don't want to go back . . . because . . . going back is . . . isolation, it's withdrawing. [22]

She is struggling here, not wanting those old feelings of withdrawal and isolation to be here with Michael. She speaks of desperately wanting to be more real, but now leaves the present moment (where I believe the new moment of gestalt could happen) and returns to a past moment, and feels stuck again:

> . . . I did not want to crack open in the church. [*nervous laugh*] But what would it have mattered . . . if I'd cried out loud? There's a conflict about everything. [*pause*] I'm not totally free . . . [22]

I experience the spirit of this key sentence very strongly. I find this intense, poignant and desperate. I feel again most puzzled by Michael's response, which begins:

> Yes, I think the question that you posed slightly changes in the posing of it . . . [22 M.J.]

Once again I find this is far too long. It seems to me too intellectual. I myself would stay more closely aligned to her own experiencing and immediacy.

Anger and self-restraint: An exploration of Michael's underlying experience

Is the issue and difficulty of developing more trust simply Ruth's private business, or might it have a great deal to do with how Michael is feeling and behaving? Might it be that Michael is in some way impeding Ruth's progress, actually being untrustworthy for Ruth? In order to explore this question, I see the purpose in supervision now to be one in which we (Michael and I) explore very thoroughly, with all the honesty and self-awareness available to Michael, precisely what is happening inside him, bringing to consciousness all possible origins of his underlying self-restraint which is so palpable to me during this session.

Let us look here at Michael's responses to some of my questions to see whether these in fact tell us more about what he is experiencing. I focus now on his response to my Questions 9 and 10, in which he makes some of the following comments:

> My main negative feelings are irritation, sometimes more intense anger, when she pushes at me to give me more. (Question 9)

> I am most conscious of my *working* with her rather than *feeling* a lot . . . I am also aware as I get into this question that there is a lot more of this type of feeling in me than I was aware of before you asked me the question. It tends to get submerged beneath the wish to work well. (Question 9)

I am intrigued by these statements. I understand Michael to be saying here that he is more aware of his preoccupation with working well, than he is of feeling very much at all. However, it seems he *is* clearly feeling a great deal, that some of this feeling is 'negative' and has therefore been kept rather safely underground. If this 'negative' element can be thoroughly vented in supervision, I sense that the stuckness caused by this 'repression' may be dissolved and a fresh way forward revealed, which may or may not include the decision to share these feelings with the client. Michael continues to explore his irritation, which develops into anger and some considerable resentment with Ruth:

> My anger likewise is one which I have to allow myself to get in touch with. I think I do not betray it to her in the way I relate to her in the session – if anything, I suspect I compensate for it by becoming more giving than some therapists would be. (Question 10)

Now it seems Michael is acknowledging his anger. However, I think we can safely assume that although he says he thinks he doesn't 'betray this to her', that these submerged feelings will have been *profoundly* affecting and influencing his behaviour. They are clearly preventing him from being congruent, in as much as he is experiencing irritation, anger and frustration, and yet behaving generously. I am sure this incongruence is being perceived by Ruth at some level. Indeed, this incongruence may have a great deal to do with the coldness and lack of comfort she talks about experiencing, which result in crossed wires and a kind of circle which reinforces itself: Michael feels angry/this is concealed from Ruth/she experiences a certain lack of relationship with Michael/she becomes more demanding/this he finds more irritating/he behaves coolly to conceal his negative feelings from her. So here is a kind of vicious circle, in which Michael communicates incongruence and self-restraint under the guise of generosity. This contradiction is hidden perhaps even from himself inside his extensive and long responses, which have the appearance of being generous and communicative; and Ruth becomes more demanding, which I believe she may be projecting into her desire for hugs and comfort. This circle perhaps demonstrates the likely hidden dialogue behind the spoken dialogue.

Another response of Michael's amplifies further the degree of his resentment:

> But I am aware sometimes, when the pressure from her is at its height, to speak more, to give her solutions, hug her or whatever, that in me there is a voice which says: 'Bloody hell – I give you an hour, not 45 minutes, I see you for £22 not £25, I see you as a private client when I don't see anyone else in that way'. And I guess such feelings do influence the way I am as a therapist, although I can only see the compensatory mechanism in me, reacting against such feelings by continuing to be generous. (Question 10)

'Reacting against' is, I feel the key phrase. It is evident to me that this reaction against his own irritation and anger is contributing centrally to the circle I spoke about above. When a therapist experiences one feeling, and reacts against it by expressing something else (e.g. compensatory generosity), he is being incongruent, in that there will now be a developing discrepancy between what is felt versus what is expressed. I believe this state of being, this discrepancy, will be perceived and experienced by his client, and that this lack of authenticity in him as a therapist will very likely depreciate the sense of safety in the relationship, which is so crucial for therapeutic change.

A deeper exploration of the origin of Michael's resentments here is critical. I feel this especially in the light of the final quotation above, in which it is evident that the particular issues of the time, money and place of therapy, about which Michael expresses his resentment, are not in any way in Ruth's power. If he offered or agreed these conditions, then he solely must be responsible for his subsequent feelings.

Touch: The past versus the present and future

When I asked Michael what he felt would be the particular questions he would bring to the supervision session, he replied:

> It is partly about the question of touch, or as Ruth puts it, 'I want a hug' – a phrase which grates on me. But I suppose it is also about how to be empathic and yet at the same time not do anything which could be experienced as abusive. (Question 11)

Michael is extremely honest in his response here. However, on the one hand he talks about having a 'position' on touch, and on the other he is highly ambivalent. It is this ambivalence that draws my attention, as I suspect it must be affecting Ruth, just as I feel sure his hidden irritation is also affecting Ruth.

> I would normally have no doubt at all that I would not touch a client in the course of therapy – occasionally, I might shake hands with a client who insists on it, or touch an arm as they leave. I have not been averse to embracing a client at the end of the last session. Indeed, I wish that I could do this with Ruth in a way that was not artificial (as I experience my response to her wish for a hug from me would be if I fell in with it), but would be genuine and spontaneous. But otherwise it is 'no touch', certainly no comforting by an arm round a shoulder or holding a hand. I am very firm on that. (Question 14)

Now I am puzzled. Is Ruth really wanting physical contact or could it be that this wish for a hug is somehow symbolic of her emotional needs? That is, might it be that Michael is behaving coolly and with self-restraint, evidenced in his long responses, mostly rather heady and intellectual in nature, and is not staying (except occasionally) very closely alongside her immediate experiencing, and that consequently Ruth is missing the safety and warmth she wants? Therefore, her need for safety, comfort and closeness becomes accentuated and symbolized in her expressed need for hugs. She then grows more demanding, and we are once more back in the same circle I spoke about above.

In other words, when alive and well the therapeutic alliance actually creates a kind of 'psychic holding' or containment in which past pain can be fully re-experienced, and new ways forward which are *not* based on the wounding of the past can actually materialize. In the transcript [18], Ruth seems to me to allude to an extremely important distinction between the pain, neglect and lack of comfort she suffered in the past, and the potential 'holding place' that therapy may provide. She talks initially about her lack of trust of Michael and then about her resistance, and ponders as to why she experiences resistance to releasing this old pain:

> And I don't quite know what that resistance is. And I still don't know. I said it was the psychotherapy first of all, because I know I'm not going to receive comfort from you in the same way. But I also know that you're trustworthy, you're safe . . . um . . . in holding whatever I give. [18]

This is a very important statement. I feel profoundly puzzled about Michael's long and extended response (on this occasion almost twice as long as hers), which begins: 'I don't know whether this is it at all . . .' [18 M.J.]. If I could frame a possible response of my own, it might be:

> It sounds like you feel confused and ambivalent about trusting me with the full extent of your past pain . . . yet you also feel a certain safety of knowing I will hold whatever you give . . . yet it is still hard to let it out . . . Is it something like this?

It seems to me that a clearer distinction somehow needs to be made between the past and the present. If Michael could trust Ruth to participate in making this distinction with him, and could more fully trust himself, then a 'hug', or some kind of touch in the present, would be less 'loaded'.

I sense there is a confusion of two issues, which may be causing extra 'loading' about physical contact. The first is the distinction between the *holding space of therapy* and any kind of *physical holding*; and the second, the *pain of the past* as distinct from the *promise of a future that is not based on re-abuse and distrust*, but on new principles of shared responsibility, self-esteem, mutuality and trust. I feel that these distinctions are not very explicit in the session, perhaps compounding Michael's feelings of ambivalence, and resulting in an extra loading being attributed to touch in the present. It seems to me that Michael is blocked from genuine/congruent expression of concern and caring in the present towards Ruth, and Ruth is at present unable to find a real release from the past.

Catch-22

The whole issue of the past versus the present seems to arise again in the final moments of the session, when Michael makes a response

which I found confusing at the beginning, but which resulted in a
very coherent sentence:

> What you want to do is to get to the stage when that
> transferring doesn't interfere with life outside. [22 M.J.]

To this Ruth replies:

> Yes . . . yeah. Yes, actually, that's quite a positive way of
> looking at it. [*pause*] Because if it isn't transferred in here . . .
> huh! . . . you wouldn't have a job to do. [*little laugh*]. [23]

The reason I like Michael's above response [23 M.J.] is its encouragement of the way forward. However, I would argue that Michael's
subsequent expression of ambivalence when Ruth asks for a hug at
the end of the session may really be putting her into a 'catch-22'.
The way forward, apparently, is agreed by both Michael and Ruth to
be one in which the past need not be re-created, and instead she
might dare to trust herself more fully. Might one say that Ruth's
inclination to give Michael a hug could be seen as her daring to
trust herself in the present, and to take that leap over the open
space in her earlier metaphor? If Michael is driven by repetitive
ambivalence and distrusts her motivation, then I suggest he is in
danger of reinforcing the earlier 'transferring' issue, almost working
against her present inclination to move forward with trust.

Many of my comments on touch are based on a very different
theoretical position to Michael's. I, too, consider the issue to be
indeed a highly sensitive one, and on balance I am inclined towards
reserve. I have worked with some long-term clients (4–6 years) with
whom I have never exchanged any physical gesture whatsoever; and
I have had other clients with whom I have felt it to be crucial that
I risk offering some gesture of touch; or I have responded to an
initiative from them for some kind of touch, be it holding hands or
an embrace. These gestures would convey for me the spirit or meaning of support, encouragement, genuine affection, or companionship
in the present, and not the meeting of some earlier unmet primal
need of my client. I suspect I have only risked touching in the moments when I have made the judgement that the meaning of my
gesture is most unlikely to be misconstrued.

I see psychotherapy as often being a space in which a client may
experience or go through the pain of past neglect; and the therapist
who tries consciously, or unconsciously, to meet the past need in
the present, rather than stand alongside his client in facing her own
past, runs the risk of neurotic collusion, and of losing his therapeutic power altogether.

I have not in any way come to this position lightly, and I am acutely aware particularly where sexual abuse has featured in the past, that any physical gesture can be very risky, as this healing space may so very easily be viewed by the client as a re-abusing space. However, bearing in mind the delicacy of this issue, I believe that as therapists in the present climate of heightened awareness of abuse that we must continue to trust ourselves with our own congruence, integrity and authenticity, daring to be bold when our judgement so instructs us, and not fall prey to fears and distrust. To fall prey thus, would result I fear in the loss of the art of psychotherapy as the truly human encounter which I believe it to be.

Guidance for the future course of therapy

First, I want to encourage Michael to explore with me his frustration and anger, which will probably involve looking at his boundary issues. As a result, I will explore with Michael whether or not he wishes or feels able to bring the fruits of this discussion back to Ruth. Here I am in hypothetical country, since I have no idea what our discussion would reveal.

Second, I want to advise Michael to shorten his own responses to Ruth. He could even suggest to Ruth that she tries to allow more frequent space in her dialogue with him, which might enable him to stay alongside her rather more than I sense he managed to do during this session.

Third, I wish to encourage an exploration with me as to *his* own feelings about sexuality, both in general terms and then quite specifically with respect to *his* actual sexual feelings towards Ruth. This whole area, I feel, needs to be opened out in supervision, and is I believe especially important when working with a person who has experienced past sexual abuse.

In this context, I *might* encourage him, further down the road in the therapy, to trust himself and her, with respect to some kind of physical gesture. Any gesture of touch, however, could only take place with the prospect of a positive and healing outcome, if Michael felt able to talk with Ruth fully about this. Clearly, this discussion cannot take place, unless or until Michael is willing to unravel thoroughly *his* part in his 'negative' feelings, since I am interested in encouraging him to increase his own genuineness and authenticity, first with himself and then with Ruth.

Conclusion

On reflection, I am struck by the following. First, I feel reinforced in my own belief about the *centrality of the relationship* between client and therapist. On the face of it, I expect all therapists would agree or pay lip service to this statement. However, I believe that the discipline and rigour of the core conditions deeply honours this truth in tangible ways which I have *not* found evidenced in other theoretical orientations. The core conditions provide not only a firm foundation and a discipline of method, but also a reliable reference point to return to, if in pursuing my own individual style and self-expression I may wander a little astray.

I admire Ruth's courage, evidenced both in the actual session and in her willingness to allow this material to be studied in this way, and subsequently to go into print. I shall be fascinated to know how her therapy proceeded. I wish her well in her future development.

I am confirmed in my belief that this work of psychotherapy is indeed demanding in the extreme, and is indeed no 'game for the faint-hearted'. Therapy challenges all therapists in the realm of intimacy, in ways we least expect, especially if we incorrectly assume that risk-taking is the sole prerogative of the client. I am reminded of Sheldon Kopp's wonderful metaphorical description of the alchemical quality of mystery as the arena in which relationship takes place:

> I imply to those with whom I sit that I am like a safety net. They may dare risk tiptoeing themselves out upon that tight-wire over the unknown and be re-assured that even, if their terror slips them and they plummet downward, all they will suffer is a rubber ball bouncing until they can right themselves again. But what of me? As I give up each worn-out piece of technique and venture forth to discover the limits of myself and therapy, the other person may be shocked to find me approaching him at those heights from the other end of the wire. At those times we may both wonder: Who is tending the net?
>
> (Kopp 1971:15)

Further reading

Buber, M. (1958). *I and Thou*. New York: Scribner.

Carotenuto, A. (1988). *The Difficult Art: A Critical Discourse on Psychotherapy*. Wilmette, IL: Chiron Publications.

Hawkins, P. and Shohet, R. (1989). *Supervision in the Helping Professions*. Buckingham: Open University Press.

Hillman, J. (1967). *Insearch: Psychology and Religion*. Dallas, TX: Spring Publications.

Kopp, S.B. (1971). *Metaphors from a Psychotherapist. Guru*. Pallo Alto, CA: Science and Behavior Books Inc.

Mearns, D. and Thorne, B. (1988). *Person-Centred Counselling in Action*. London: Sage.

Rogers, C.R. (1951). *Client-Centred Therapy*. London: Constable.

Rogers, C.R. (1980). *A Way of Being*. Boston, MA: Houghton Mifflin.

Villas-Boas Bowen, M.C. (1986). Personality differences and person-centred supervision. *Person-Centred Review*, Vol. 1, No. 3, pp. 291–309.

6 MELANIE FENNELL

COGNITIVE-BEHAVIOUR THERAPY

The supervisor

I am a consultant clinical psychologist working in adult mental health for Oxfordshire Mental Healthcare NHS Trust at the Warneford Hospital, Oxford. I am director of a one-year part-time post-qualification multi-professional course in cognitive therapy, upon which I both train and supervise. I am also a member of a research team in the Oxford University Department of Psychiatry, developing cognitive models and treatments for anxiety disorders.

My original training was behavioural. I first encountered cognitive therapy in 1979 when I came to Oxford to take part in a clinical outcome trial of cognitive therapy for depression, then quite new to the UK. I was impressed by cognitive therapy's effectiveness in a problem area previously relatively closed to structured psychological interventions. I was also struck by the potential range and flexibility of the approach – its ability to help not only with depression, but with other problem areas and with issues arising in therapy, including the client's reactions to therapy and to the therapist and indeed my reactions to the client. I found clients liked cognitive therapy's openness and equality, and that the model it is based on made sense to them. I was attracted by its reflexivity, which meant that learning the approach also meant growth in personal understanding.

I began designing and leading workshops in cognitive therapy for depression in the early 1980s, and found teaching practical skills both stimulating and fun. My interest in training and supervision has grown from there.

First reactions to the transcript

My first reaction was that this session was a 'golden moment' in therapy when issues from the past, events in the here-and-now and aspects of the therapeutic encounter all came together in more or less perfect synchrony. What an opportunity! I was struck by Michael's evident awareness of these overlapping patterns, and could recognize how he worked to encourage Ruth to focus on the central issues of trust and exposure, how these had been triggered by recent events, how those events echoed past confusions of caring and abuse, and how these were playing out in the interaction with him. I was struck also by the evident closeness and solidity of the therapeutic relationship, the depth of his knowledge and understanding of Ruth, and the extent to which (even at this difficult moment) she clearly felt able to confide in him.

I have to admit also to a sense of frustration: Michael has all this information, but what is he doing with it? I was longing for him to move from insight to active change. I felt Ruth was champing at the bit (especially towards the end of the session), that she had the courage to try operating differently (after all, she has confronted her fears about him by coming) – and then nothing happened! The session finished with both therapist and client clear about the issues, but no real sense of direction or movement, or impression that the session had been used as a jumping-off point from which to question old rules for living, reinterpret the present in more realistic and helpful terms, or set up plans for thinking and acting differently in the future.

This was the cognitive-behaviourist in me, looking for structure, clear goals and a pattern of systematic interventions, agreed between therapist and client and designed not simply to elucidate repeating patterns in the present and their origins in early life, but also to work collaboratively towards change, interweaving cognitive and behavioural strategies so as to maximize the client's chances of seeing her world differently, and acting and thinking differently within that new perspective.

Further information

The main things in my mind after reading the transcript were: curiosity about Ruth's reasons for moving from a technical line of work to one requiring considerable self-analysis and (albeit structured) intimacy; curiosity about Michael's reasons for choosing as subject for this exercise a client with concerns about exposure and abuse; and a question as to where Michael thought therapy was going, what his and Ruth's goals were, and how they would decide when enough had been done and it was time to stop.

The last of these was most important as a supervision point, since I suspected that this treatment, now eighteen months in duration, might not be guided by concrete, explicit goals, openly shared by client and therapist, with regular monitoring of progress. If so, I thought it possible that neither Ruth nor Michael might have a clear idea of how far they had come, where they should go next, or exactly what they were aiming at. This issue will be returned to in the main body of the chapter. The only point I wish to remark on here is that my original impression was confirmed by Michael in his response to one of my questions: 'Part of me at that time could not see an end to it – I think there was a feeling of some despair that things did not seem to be getting anywhere for her'.

Detailed comments on the session

Introduction

I write this commentary as if Michael (and the reader) were an aspiring cognitive therapist, which is of course unfair, since cognitive therapy was not what Michael was intending to do. By 'cognitive therapy' I mean the model of emotional disorder and associated treatment paradigm originally defined by A.T. Beck. I think that writing from this perspective will allow me to show clearly how far what Michael is doing overlaps with, and is different from, what I would expect of a typical cognitive therapy session at this point in treatment. It will also allow me to combine specific comments on content and style with a certain amount of teaching and information-giving about the nature of cognitive therapy, which I would normally expect to do with a therapist at this stage of development. I found the transcript and the audiotape of the session extremely helpful. They provided information on the content and process of the session far more vivid, detailed and accurate than a verbal report; indeed, listening to and giving detailed feedback on therapy tapes is a routine part of supervision in cognitive therapy. The benefit is that I can comment not only on the therapist's overall understanding of Ruth's position and his broad strategy for change ('working through' as Michael described it in a covering letter), but also on how their interaction proceeds from moment to moment, and the exact nature of his intervention at each point. My first suggestion as supervisor to Michael is that, in the interests of extending his skills, he begins regularly to audiotape therapy sessions and to listen to the tapes. This will help him to pinpoint his strengths and weaknesses as a cognitive therapist and to identify aspects of his performance which he wishes to improve. As a guideline for what he should be aiming at, I suggest that he use the Cognitive Therapy Scale, a standardized measure of competence in cognitive therapy (Freeman *et al.*, 1990).

My normal practice when giving feedback on a particular session is to provide a very detailed blow-by-blow analysis of the session, interspersing an abbreviated transcript with questions, comments and suggestions for change. There is not space here for that. I should like instead to focus my comments around three main topics: case conceptualization, the style and structure of treatment, and the need for therapist and client to use their joint understanding of the development and maintenance of Ruth's difficulties as a starting point for active change. In each section, I start with some general points to orientate the therapist and give him a sense of what he should be aiming at. I shall follow this with specific points relevant to Ruth, and practical suggestions for developing the therapist's skills and improving his competence as a cognitive therapist.

First, a general point: cognitive therapy has a tradition of working within the 'scientist practitioner' model. This means that clinical work is informed by and reciprocally informs theory-building and research. In practical terms, this means that Michael will need to familiarize himself with the literature so that his practice will be in line with the latest developments on the theoretical and clinical front. Later, he may wish to contribute to that literature himself, as his experience grows. There is a brief list of key references at the end of the chapter.

Case conceptualization

The role of the cognitive model

Cognitive therapy is based on a coherent theoretical model of emotional disorder. More broadly, the cognitive model can be seen as a way of understanding how people function. It applies not only to people meeting formal diagnostic criteria for psychiatric disorders (although these are the clients for whom it was originally designed), but also to clients in a more general sense, and indeed to ourselves and how we respond to everyday events in our lives. Thus the model assumes continuity between people seeking help for emotional difficulties and people at large – one of its attractive characteristics to my mind.

The model suggests that, on the basis of early experience, we form beliefs or assumptions about ourselves, other people and the world. These assumptions then shape how we perceive, interpret and respond to subsequent experience. This means that they tend to be self-maintaining, in that we see what we are primed to see, and ignore or discount information which does not fit our preconceived ideas. Some assumptions are absolute: for example, 'I am no good', 'People are untrustworthy'. Absolute assumptions are often called 'core beliefs' or 'schemas'. Some dysfunctional assumptions are conditional: for example, 'If I do what people want, then they will like me', or 'Unless I always control my feelings, I will fall apart'. Assumptions, whether absolute or conditional, are 'dysfunctional' in that they are extreme, rigid and resistant to change. They are said to create vulnerability to distress or emotional disorder when the person encounters situations of direct relevance to them (critical incidents). So, for example, if I believe success is crucial to my self-worth, I am likely to become distressed in the face of failure. If, on the other hand, I believe that it is essential always to be loved, then the loss or absence of love would be my trigger point for distress. Once activated, dysfunctional assumptions give rise to what Beck has called 'negative automatic thoughts', negative in that they are associated with unpleasant emotions, and automatic in that they 'pop into people's heads', rather than being the product of any sort of reasoning process. Negative automatic thoughts occur in specific situations, and may take the form of words, images in the mind's eye, or implicit meanings. The model suggests that they are a prime influence on people's feelings and behaviour. In therapy, they are normally the initial target for change, followed later in treatment by the dysfunctional assumptions on which they are based.

Developing an individual case conceptualization

The conceptualization is the point where theory meets practice, where the generic cognitive model of emotional disorder is tailored specifically to the individual client and is used to guide the progress of therapy. The cognitive therapist's task is to discover how the information presented by the client, including reports of outside events past and present and also responses to therapist and to therapy, can be understood in terms of the model. That is, the cognitive therapist has constantly in mind the question, 'Where does this fit?' He or she attempts, as treatment progresses, to draw up a conceptualization or map of the territory that will satisfactorily explain: (a) the immediate difficulties the client is experiencing (thoughts, feelings and behaviour, including reactions to therapy and therapist); (b) the events which trigger their distress on a day-to-day basis and which sparked off their difficulties in the first place; (c) the underlying cognitive vulnerability which made those events particularly significant for them (their dysfunctional assumptions); and (d) the experiences, often in early childhood, which gave rise to psychological vulnerability in the first place and have reinforced it over time. The conceptualization among other things allows us to predict the kind of difficulties we might expect in therapy with particular clients, for example, issues of trust or the need to be wholly autonomous or to please.

The process of developing a conceptualization is necessarily dynamic and evolving, since clients are constantly providing us with new information that we must make sense of and 'fit in'. If we cannot do so, this is a sign that we are not on the right track and need to re-think our perspective. Additionally, the conceptualization is not the property of the therapist but is explicitly shared with the client. This helps clients to make sense of their experiences, awakens their curiosity and encourages them to share fully in the process of understanding and change.

Ruth's conceptualization

The session transcript shows that Michael already has in mind a conceptualization of Ruth's current difficulties. He relates them to previous experience, shows how they have been triggered by recent events, and explores how they emerge in her feelings and thoughts about the current session. He repeatedly refers to his overall understanding of how her problems have developed, and he shares his perceptions with Ruth. Equally it is clear that she is actively engaged in the process of making links between different aspects of her experience.

The difference in cognitive therapy proper, I think, would be in the degree of structure placed on this information, and in the fact that the understanding expressed in the conceptualization would be explicitly presented as a first step towards active, systematic change procedures. The conceptualization should be written down, with each person retaining a copy. Session to session, both keep this in front of them so that when related issues arise they can turn to it together and ask: 'Where does this fit? How can we make sense of what just happened? Which of your beliefs or assumptions was triggered then? What earlier experiences might this be reminding you of? What are the feelings, thoughts, behaviours and body sensations in play right now?' Thus the conceptualization forms the basis for the client achieving an initial distance from the hurly-burly of everyday experience: 'Aha! Here I go again. Here's that old thing again. I may not be able to do much about it now, but at least I can see it for what it is'.

Based on the information Michael has provided, Ruth's conceptualization might look something like that in Fig. 1. Necessarily this is based on limited information, and may well omit or be inaccurate about particular elements. Michael is in a good position to make corrections, and of course Ruth is in an even better position.

The conceptualization allows the therapist to make the process of 'transferring' clear and explicable. It makes sense of apparently illogical reactions (for example, to the recent operation) by showing how similarities between current trigger situations and previous experience will activate systems which were appropriate and healthy at an earlier stage (if you are being abused, it makes sense to be wary; if abuse gives you the closeness and comfort you need, it makes sense to feel confused about where caring stops and violation starts), but may now be over-generalized, rigid anachronisms, no longer in line with the reality of current circumstances. This both normalizes current distresses and opens an avenue for change. It encourages the client to tune into the detail of immediate reactions to current situations (thoughts, feelings, body sensations and behaviours), and to begin to stand back and systematically question the accuracy of perceptions and interpretations of experience ('What's running through my mind right now? What's my evidence for thinking what I do? How far is this situation actually similar to past experiences which it reminds me of? How far and in what ways is it different? How am I different from the little girl who was abused? What do I need to do to change the situation? Or to change my reactions to it?', etc.). In the current session, examples of situations that might benefit from this kind of detailed exploration would be Ruth's fears of coming to see Michael on the day of the session, and her reactions when she realized what must have happened during the operation.

Practical points for the therapist

1 Michael needs to draw up a conceptualization; to take time before the next meeting to review all the information he has (including what he knows about Ruth's past, current events that are discussed week to week, and her reactions to him and to therapy); and to pull it together in the form of a flowchart similar to the one shown in Fig. 1. He should indicate any gaps with a '?' With this flowchart, he can ask himself the following questions:

• Does this conceptualization account satisfactorily for all the information he has?

Early experience
Little support/encouragement from parents/brother – distant, critical
Sexual interference from brother. Rape age 8 by brother's friends
No help from mother – grow up, don't be silly – felt ignored, uncared for
Abuse mixed with closeness/physical contact I needed – confusion
↓
Absolute assumptions (schemas)
Men are dangerous/abusive/take advantage of vulnerability
I am vulnerable (?not good enough? not important?)
No-one can be trusted
No-one cares about me, or will look after or protect me
↓
Conditional assumptions
If I let people get close, they will hurt or abuse me
I must always keep people at a distance
If I am not in control, I am not safe
The only way to get closeness or comfort is to expose myself to abuse
↓
Critical incidents
Originally: Road accident, orderly's reaction, parents' slowness to visit
Now: Treated as second best by mother, circumstances of redundancy,
illness/no visitors or signs of care, operation and its aftermath, not
being given affection/comfort by Michael
↓
Negative automatic thoughts
I want to be cared for and comforted
Who can I trust?
Not even Michael will give me what I want
Where will it all end? Will I ever be able to trust anyone?

Emotions   *Body sensations*
Vulnerable, exposed, sad   Cold
Angry, frustrated   Tense, uptight
Frightened, alienated   Tearful

Behaviour
Withdraw from people, hide feelings,
avoid close relationships, cry

Strengths/assets/qualities
Courage, persistence, hard worker, articulate, self-aware, ability to
make a career, ability to make positive relationships (Frank, Brian,
Michael)

Implications for therapy (possible points of difficulty)
Wanting to be held, loved, make love, give love, temptation to break
boundaries
Anger/frustration when needs not met
Difficulty trusting/tolerating closeness
Likely to see therapist as untrustworthy, cold, critical

Figure 1   Ruth's conceptualization

- Are there contradictions or inconsistencies? What are they? What extra information does he need? How can he get it?
- Do the absolute and conditional assumptions identified make sense in terms of the experiences on which they were based? That is, would anyone who had had these experiences be likely to come to similar conclusions?
- Do the events triggering distress now 'fit' the assumptions he has identified? Are they the sort of events he might expect to distress someone holding those particular beliefs? How far do they match early experience?
- In situations Ruth finds problematic, what is her immediate response? For example, when she was waiting to see him that day, what exactly was running through her mind, word for word? What images were in her mind's eye? What emotions exactly was she experiencing (sad, frightened, alienated, etc.)? And what about her body state (for example, several times during the session she mentions feeling 'cold')? Finally, what did she actually do (what was her behavioural response)?

He should try the same exercise (precise mapping of the phenomenology) in relation to waking after the operation, lying awake in the night, and standing on the platform in the tree. Are there particular aspects of her experience that are very clear to him, but others that he does not regularly explore? What are they? From now on he will need to draw up this sort of mini-map delineating immediate reactions each time they both focus on a particular upsetting situation. It will help both of them to be clear about the phenomenology of Ruth's distress, and about the relationship between particular thoughts, feelings, body sensations and behaviours in specific situations. This in turn will help them both to develop their skill at spotting repeating patterns that mark the activation of dysfunctional assumptions.

2 As I have already suggested, the conceptualization is to be shared and there is no time like the present! When Michael next meets Ruth, let him set aside part of the session to feed back to her the way he has pulled together all the information she has given him, so that she will have an opportunity to reflect on the picture he presents and to judge how far it is accurate and helpful. She will also be able to help him with inconsistencies and with gaps in his knowledge. Michael could introduce the topic something like this:

I have been thinking about everything you have told me about yourself, and trying to pull it all together and make sense of it. We have been doing this to some extent as we have gone along

– now I should like to see if together we can draw up a map that will make sense of your experiences. This is based on what you have told me, but I realize that there may well be things I have left out or got wrong, and it would be very helpful to me to have your ideas as we go through it so that I can be sure I am understanding things correctly. How does that sound to you?

The idea then is to go through the draft, chunk by chunk, interspersing what he says with regular requests for Ruth's reactions ('What sense does that make to you? What's your reaction to that idea? How far does this match what you have thought yourself?', etc.). Presenting the conceptualization is not a lecture on the therapist's part, but a gradual exploration of their understanding of what she has told him, with open encouragement to point out where he has gone wrong, where she disagrees with him, and where he has understood her correctly.

At the end of the session, he can then take the second draft they have produced together, and make one copy for each of them. Ruth's task before meeting again will be to reflect on what they have produced, and to assess where there are gaps that she can fill, what fits and what does not fit. The therapist should ask her in particular to be watchful for things that are wrong with the conceptualization – this is the information that will be most helpful to him in gaining an accurate understanding of her. He can then discuss the ideas that she comes up with next time they meet. After that, the conceptualization will become a map to guide exploration and change, being modified where necessary as new information emerges.

The style of therapy

'Collaborative empiricism' is the term used to describe the therapeutic relationship in cognitive therapy. 'Empiricism' I shall return to later; 'collaboration' is my focus here. In practice, there are three principal things to keep in mind as far as the style and structure of the therapeutic encounter are concerned: rapport building, active collaboration and treatment structure.

Rapport building

This means the fundamentals of a good therapeutic relationship, which apply just as strongly in cognitive therapy as in counselling (i.e. accurate empathy, non-possessive warmth and genuineness). I do not think cognitive therapy has anything to teach Michael here.

He has a gentle, caring style which respects Ruth's perspective and cuts through her initial prickliness and fear to facilitate the expression of central issues. He is highly adept at reflecting not only the overt content of what she says, but also the feelings and confusions expressed or implied, and in many cases underlying issues that she does not make explicit. He treats her with respect and is careful not to impinge or impose – especially important, given her history. He comes over as friendly, warm and accepting, with a confident sincerity and professionalism. The end result is clearly evident in the degree to which Ruth, for whom trust is an issue, trusts the therapist, even to the point of confiding the boundaries of her trust.

Active collaboration

In cognitive therapy, client and therapist are engaged together as a team, first in exploring immediate thinking and underlying assumptions, and then in actively working to change them. Working as a team means that a therapist needs to be explicit about what he or she does, and about the reasons for doing it. For example:

> What I should like to do now is to find out more about what exactly was running through your mind when you were waiting to see me today, and how that affected you. This is so that we can discover what the issues were, how they link up with other events we have discussed here, and what you can do differently if something similar comes up again. How does that sound to you?

The final question here, a request for feedback on the suggestion made, is also characteristic of team working. Michael needs to get into the habit of matching his skill at ensuring that he is tracking what the patient says (reflection) by following any suggestion on his part with a request for feedback on understanding (e.g. 'What do you think I am suggesting here?') and on response (e.g. 'What's your reaction to that idea?'). I think in fact he does this implicitly through pauses, hesitations, repetitions and dysfluencies, and by making his suggestions very tentative. Examples would be: 'I'm not sure whether it's something I've said or done, or . . . or whether it's what's been happening to you' [**3** M.J.]; 'You would need to tell me whether this is right or not' [**4** M.J.]; 'I don't know whether this is it at all . . . and helps, but let's try it and see' [**18** M.J.]; 'I'm not sure whether this helps or not really' [**21** M.J.]. In cognitive therapy, Michael would need to be more explicit in asking for feedback, so that the patient is given a very clear message that he expects her to participate actively in what is going on and to tell him if his suggestions are inaccurate or irrelevant.

The main tool through which active collaboration proceeds is 'guided discovery'. This means in essence not empathy, reflection and interpretation on the one hand, nor directive instruction-giving on the other, but a sequence of careful questions designed to encourage clients to elucidate their experience and to seek alternative perspectives that will be more realistic (more in line with the evidence than with pre-conceived ideas) and more helpful. Typically, therapist utterances in cognitive therapy are relatively brief. The lack of questions is one of the most striking shortcomings of the recorded session as far as cognitive therapy is concerned. In the whole session, Michael asks only ten questions. Of these, four are requests for further information: 'Can you tell me? Can you express more of the alienation?' [2 M.J.]; 'That means you felt shivery?' [12 M.J.]; 'Do you feel angry about that?' [13 M.J.]. Three questions are mainly bridging manoeuvres, closed questions expecting the answer 'yes': 'Sounds like more than that, doesn't it?' [3 M.J.]; 'Do you know what I mean?' [4 M.J.]; 'It's a very motherly gesture, isn't it?' [15 M.J.]. Only three questions read like real attempts to explore meaning more deeply or to move towards a change in perspective: 'What would happen? Where would it lead?' [18 M.J.]; 'What *do* you say to the kids that you take on that assault course, if they hesitate?' [21 M.J.]. The last of the three is the only one where Michael gives Ruth time to respond; the other two are rhetorical. Most of his utterances convey his understanding of meaning, or links that he draws between different aspects of experience; that is, meaning and associations are supplied by the therapist, rather than elicited from Ruth. This is not to say that Michael in any sense imposes his views on Ruth; indeed, his approach is careful and tentative, allowing plenty of space for her to disagree, as indeed she does on occasion. Neither do I wish to suggest that his comments are off course. On the contrary, he shows great skill in homing in on what cognitive therapy calls the 'hot' topics – live issues associated with high affect, which is where the action is in therapy. However, the lack of questioning means that the therapist does not explicitly encourage Ruth to explore in more detail or more deeply the meaning of her experience, and to come to conclusions and reach alternative perspectives for herself.

Taking some examples from the transcript and suggesting guided discovery alternatives might most clearly illustrate what I mean (see Fig. 2). I should add that it is important to intersperse questions of this kind with reflections, statements of empathy, capsule summaries and so forth. Cognitive therapy is not meant to sound like the Spanish Inquisition!

Original	Guided discovery alternative
Section 3: 'It's as though . . . or whether it's what's been happening to you'.	Can we pinpoint when these feelings started? When you started feeling that way, what was running through your mind? Where does this fit with our overall understanding of your difficulties?
Section 4: 'What I'm struck by is . . . neither of them are actually at all pleasant'.	What is it about me being a psychotherapist which makes it hard for you to talk? And what about me being a man? How similar is this to how you have been feeling over the last few days? What does this remind you of? Which assumptions of yours might be triggered here?
Section 5: 'I think the man bit is . . . that makes it actually very hard'.	When you think about sharing with me, what comes into your mind? What if you did? What are you afraid might happen? What might I do? What is the worst thing that might follow?
Section 10: 'It also sounds from what you're saying . . . comforting, holding, healing'.	What does that dream mean to you? What might Brian represent? And me? What is it about faith that meets your needs just now? And what is different about therapy? And about me?
Sections 12–13: R: 'Yeah, I did feel that was OK . . .'. M.J.: 'Do you feel angry about that?'	Do you have an image in your mind's eye of what happened? Could you tell me about it? Supposing you were touched and so on, what does that mean to you? What does it say about you? About other people? When you think about what happened, how do you feel? What does this feeling remind you of? When have you had that cold feeling before?
Section 15: 'Yes. I wonder whether this sort of builds on . . . at the same time you'd like it'.	How does that link up with what we've been discussing? What did the surgeon's kindness mean to you? How come that was OK at that point? What made it safe? What was the difference later? What

makes control so important – what would happen if you did *not* have it? How does that link up with how things are in other relationships? And here? How does that link up with what you felt before our session today?

Section 18: 'I don't know whether this is at all . . . both keep away and also be close'.

What would happen if you *did* let it out? How might I react? What would it feel like for you? What would have to be different for you to feel safe to do that? What would it mean to you if I *did* give you cuddling and loving and hugging? And what does it mean that I don't? How do you feel when I don't? And what runs through your mind? What other ways might there be for me to show caring and warmth and affection? And in other relationships, what other ways are there of showing these things?

(These same questions apply to the requests for a hug at the end of the session, and subsequently. It is possible that if Michael had followed this line of inquiry at this point, these awkwardnesses could have been avoided or at least have been attenuated by referring back to this point in the session, and reminding Ruth of other ways in which he shows he cares.)

Section 21: 'How could I complain?'

That's a very good question. How might you answer it? Supposing you heard another little girl asking that, what would your reaction be? What would you say to her? And how could you apply that to yourself?

Section 21: 'Your fear is . . .'

What if you could guarantee that that wouldn't happen? How might you feel then? How far is this what was troubling you before we met today? What is the fear if you get angry with me, or tell me you can't trust me? What might I do? What would happen to our relationship? If you think back over our session today, how far has that actually happened? What about previous sessions? How much evidence do you have that telling me how you feel has pushed me away? What evidence is there from my reactions to you that does not fit with that prediction? So next time you feel that, what could you do to test out if you are right?

Figure 2 Examples of guided discovery

Practical points

1 *Self-monitoring*. When Michael listens to the session tapes, he could take note of where he makes a meaning statement or a link or offers an interpretation? He could stop the tape at that point and ask himself: 'What question could I have asked there?' It is best to avoid closed questions which only allow the answers 'yes' or 'no'. Questions starting with 'what' or 'how' are often the most useful (see Fig. 2).

2 *Within-session change*. In therapy sessions, when Michael feels tempted to supply a meaning or a link, let him pause and see if he can find a question instead. Remember the principle in guided discovery is curiosity about the client's thinking and its effects ('What's going on here?') and about finding the best way to change things ('What can be done about it?').

3 *Develop a range of good questions*. It is helpful to develop a repertoire of useful questions. Michael can do this by monitoring his own performance (making a note of which questions seem most productive in practice), by exchanging ideas with other cognitive therapists and by reading (e.g. Fennell, in Hawton *et al*. 1989). Ultimately, the whole purpose of guided discovery is for clients to learn to question their own thinking and the interpretation they place on things. So the therapist can help the client to develop their own 'library' of questions that encourage them to identify the biases and exaggerations in their thinking and to re-evaluate how they see things and find new ways of acting in the world.

The structure of therapy

The cognitive therapist is responsible for providing a structure for therapy as a whole and for each individual session within therapy.

Overall structure

To provide a general direction for therapy, therapist and client together begin by determining the client's goals. These must be clear,
specific and achievable in the time available. A useful starting point
is often to list the client's main difficulties, and to ask in relation to
each: 'What are your goals as far as this is concerned?', 'How exactly
would you like things to be different in this area?', 'Supposing therapy worked for you, how would things have changed at the end?'
Comments made during the session and Michael's responses to my
questions indicate that focused goal-setting has not been carried out,
although both Michael and Ruth have some sense of where they are
heading – working through memories (including having an opportunity to talk through early experiences, and getting 'to the stage when
that transferring doesn't interfere with life outside'), learning to
trust, developing confidence in interpersonal relationships, finding
a loving partner. I am not clear how far these goals have been openly
acknowledged by both of them and are therefore shared.

Session structure

It appears from the transcript that the session simply flows from the
topic Ruth first presents. In cognitive therapy, sessions are structured in a rather different way, opening each session by agreeing
an 'agenda' (or list of today's topics) with the client. The rationale
for this is that there is only a limited time together, and that it
is important to ensure that the therapist deals with what is most
important to the client at that point. Novice cognitive therapists,
especially those from a psychodynamic or counselling background,
sometimes feel this will be very constraining. My own experience
is that nearly all clients can see the point of it, feel secure within
the structure that it implies, and are happy to begin the session
by suggesting their own items for discussion.

In practice, each session begins by spending a few minutes decid-
ing together what it is most important to cover today. Certain items
recur routinely week to week:

1 *Review of the previous session.* On reflection, what further reactions to the session has the client had? Are there any points that
need to be picked up? Providing the client with an audiotape of
each therapy session is invaluable here, in that the tape will act as
a memory and opportunity for reflection. The client can also have a
'therapy notebook' in which he or she records important points from
each session and make a note of questions, comments, further reflections and the like.

2 *Review of previous homework.* In essence, cognitive therapy is a self-help approach. It assumes that through therapy clients acquire the skills they need in order to manage their own affairs and resolve problems for themselves. The therapist is like a mentor or coach, teaching relevant skills and giving feedback on the client's attempts to put them into practice. Cognitive therapy recognizes that skills acquisition requires regular practice. For this reason, each session is followed by homework assignments, carrying what has been learned into the outside world. These are then discussed at the next meeting. What happened? What was learned? Were there any difficulties? How could these have been overcome? What else needs to be done? What other areas in the client's life could these skills be applied to?

Homework may include regular practice at cognitive therapy skills (for example, monitoring or questioning negative automatic thoughts) and one-off assignments (for example, experimenting with being more open with one particular person at one particular time). One-offs would generally relate to broader issues (in this case, the assumption that being open makes one vulnerable to abuse).

3 *Agreeing new homework for the following week.* Towards the end of each session, time is set aside to decide with the client what he or she might most usefully do before meeting again, in order to build on what has been achieved in the session. In this particular session, useful homework assignments might include:

- Listening to the therapy tape and noting important points.
- Recording interpersonal situations during the week where Ruth feels exposed or at risk, and describing as accurately as she can her thoughts, feelings, body sensations and behaviour (later this observation will become a basis for questioning and re-evaluating her thoughts, and later still for collecting evidence relating to underlying assumptions).
- Keeping a log of signs of caring in others, however small (her tendency is to notice signs that people do *not* care; it is possible that this is not a full or accurate picture).

4 *Session summary/request for feedback.* Before the session ends, it is important to summarize what has been covered together, and find out what the client's understanding of the session is, and how he or she feels about it. This encourages active learning on the part of the client and also facilitates collaboration. Useful questions when making the summary include: 'What have we covered today? What have you learned? What are the most important points for you to keep

in mind?' It is helpful to write down the answers to these, so that neither therapist nor client rely entirely on memory. Useful questions to tap the client's reactions to the session as a whole include: 'How do you feel about our session today? What are your reactions to what we have discussed? Was there anything difficult or upsetting? Anything you didn't like, or that didn't make sense?'

The summary of this particular session might run:

> At the beginning of our session, you were fearful of talking openly to me because I seemed cold and clinical, and perhaps because I am a man and therefore dangerous for you to expose yourself to. How do you feel about that now? How far have your fears been borne out? Did I react as you thought I would? What do you learn from that? We have discussed how these fears were triggered off by the aftermath of the operation, and we could see links between that and the original abuse, the episode after the accident, and our situation here. In each case, caring is muddled up with the possibility of exposure and violation. We talked about how difficult it is to trust, and you made it very clear how much you want to move from mistrust into a position where you feel you can trust more – a very risky business which feels like stepping into a void. How would you feel about making that change our main topic for next week? We could start by exploring whether it need be such a big step as it seems, and maybe work out some ways of taking little steps forward without exposing yourself too much. Today's session would be an example of that, you felt frightened, but you came, and you talked to me. What's your reaction to that idea?

Practical points

1 *Overall treatment structure.* Michael needs now to make the goals explicit and discuss with Ruth exactly how they may be defined, how progress towards them may be monitored and assessed, and how they will know when she has achieved them. It may seem rather odd to do this now, in mid-therapy. A possible method would be to suggest to Ruth that together they carry out a joint review of progress ('What have you learned from our sessions? What has been helpful to you? What areas need further work?'). Michael could introduce goal-setting in relation to the review, in the interests of ensuring that he is focusing on what is most important, and that together they have some clear idea of where they are heading.

The conceptualization can be introduced at the same time, and will guide the specific directions Michael and Ruth take to reach the goals. The normal pattern would be to work 'bottom up'; that is, to begin by working on specific negative automatic thoughts in specific current situations, and then to move to deal with issues at a more abstract level (assumptions) once these skills had been mastered. However, given Ruth's level of understanding and the amount of information Michael already has about her, plus her evident assets and strengths, he may well be able to proceed on both fronts at once (see section on change procedures below).

2 *Session structure.* I suggest that the therapist begins right away getting practice at structuring sessions, as suggested above. Initially, as he is not used to it, this will feel very odd and he may even feel rather 'straitjacketed', and fear that the client will feel the same. I suggest that he attempts a behavioural experiment. He can start by predicting what he thinks will happen if he tries structuring a session. Look out in particular for negative predictions like 'I won't be able to do it' or 'She won't do the homework' or 'I won't be able to be sensitive and spontaneous'. He should write the predictions down and rate how far he believes each one (0–100%). Then he should try the new way and see if the outcome fits these predictions. If not, how far now does Michael believe his original predictions (0–100%)? If his predictions prove correct, then what does he need to do differently in order to become more comfortable with working in a new way? The therapist needs to remember that he is trying something new, and that it will take a while to get used to it; in other words, it may not be reasonable to expect things to run smoothly immediately. How long is a reasonable time scale? When will he review progress? How will he go about monitoring the client's reactions to the new style?

If Michael tries this exercise, he will kill two birds with one stone: he will get a chance to hone his skills at structuring therapy time, and he will have an opportunity to try using a behavioural experiment to test out the validity of his own ideas. This is exactly what he will be expecting Ruth to do in therapy.

Using understanding as a basis for active change

Collaborative empiricism: Cognitive and behavioural change strategies

Cognitive therapy can be viewed as an experiment which therapist and client are conducting together. This is the 'empiricism' of 'collaborative empiricism'. First a hypothesis is developed about the factors accounting for the development and maintenance of current problems (the conceptualization). Then the hypothesis is tested through a series of organized interventions manipulating key variables (working to change negative automatic thoughts and assumptions). Outcome of what is done at each stage is carefully assessed, measuring changes in thinking, mood and behaviour. Similarly, the client is taught to see his or her thoughts and assumptions not as facts, but as hypotheses which are open to question and whose validity may be tested through behavioural experiments. So the change methods described below are in a sense ways of testing out clients' theories about themselves, other people and the world and examining how far these theories fit the facts and how helpful they are. The aim is to use experience to come up with new theories which will be more realistic and more helpful. Precise assessment of outcome is a way of ensuring that any new theories are good ones, with a constructive impact on how the client thinks, feels and acts on a day-to-day basis.

From the information Michael sent me, moving from insight to change seems to be the area in which both he and Ruth feel most stuck. He has a very good understanding of her difficulties, and she conveys graphically (the tree metaphor) how she would like things to be different. Neither therapist nor client, however, seem clear about where to go next. Ruth's puzzlement and frustration are vividly expressed: 'How on earth do I get out of this hole, because it's been going on for the last thirty-eight years? Almost as if the positive side of all this is that I'm making a hell of a lot of connections now. I don't like the connections I'm making, but we're making these things; and how the hell do I break the mould and be able to trust, or whatever?'

In this area, cognitive therapy has much to offer. Rather than assuming that insight will lead to recovery or growth, it has developed an extensive repertoire of change strategies, based closely on its understanding of how emotional disorder and distress develop and are maintained. In relation to the particular client, this means that the therapy strategy is guided by the individual conceptualization. The first step normally is to modify immediate interpretations of experience (negative automatic thoughts), the second to change dysfunctional assumptions on which these are based. However, in the case of Ruth, the most elegant move might be to make changes in the here-and-now within the framework of modifying background beliefs.

Ruth: The central issue

The central issue, as Ruth indicates above, is one of trust. In essence, no-one can be trusted: men are dangerous and exploitative, women are cold, uncaring and critical. It is better, therefore, to be safe than sorry – better to keep her distance. She longs for human contact, affection and comfort, but at the same time believes that allowing closeness makes her vulnerable to abuse. I do not know word for word what her assumptions might be, but let us assume 'No-one can be trusted' on the absolute level and 'If I let people get close they will hurt or abuse me' at the conditional level. The cognitive model suggests that these will be the driving force behind everyday reactions, which in turn will reinforce them. They could account for her difficulty in forming close lasting relationships, her sensitivity to any sign of violation, and the wariness she experiences with Michael, as well as her frustration when his carefully maintained clinical distance fails to meet her needs. She needs his care and support, but at the same time fears what it might lead to.

The essence of the problem seems to be that Ruth sees trust as an absolute, all-or-nothing thing: you trust people, or you do not. No half-way measures. She expresses this in her metaphor of the two trees [20], and says:

> . . . it's almost as if my two alternatives are either to go . . . and express what's going on here, be in the pain of it. Or to withdraw; there's no happy medium. It seems to be all or nothing all the time. I can't find a nice, a nice way out. [15]

This awareness of dichotomous (black and white) thinking is an excellent starting point for change in long-standing absolute and conditional assumptions and in her day-to-day reactions. That is, by introducing flexibility into her basic beliefs (more choice as to whether to trust or not), the therapist can open the way to questioning negative automatic thoughts in specific situations and to experimenting on a behavioural level with different ways of operating in personal relationships. In turn, these specific changes will feed back into changes on the assumption level.

Practical points

1 *Using continua to change assumptions.* I suggest that the therapist and client begin by considering together the nature of trust. Start by rating Ruth's belief in the statement: 'No-one can be trusted'. This seems to Ruth like a black and white matter, but how far is this actually true? Should everybody either not be trusted at all or be trusted under all circumstances to the same degree no matter who they are? It may be helpful to examine the nature of trustworthiness on a dimension, or continuum:

0 —————————————————————————————— 100
Not at all   Totally
trustworthy   trustworthy
in any way   in every way

Work out in detail what the two poles mean. Both need to be
defined in extreme terms (always/never, everything/nothing, etc.).
'Totally trustworthy' might, for example, include never being angry,
always being 100 per cent reliable and predictable, being totally
honest, being sexually sensitive, always being there when needed,
never being too tired or preoccupied to listen, etc. In other words,
never ever putting a foot wrong. 'Not at all trustworthy', by contrast, might include always being unpredictable and unreliable, never
telling the truth, wholly self-centred, abusive, etc. When the ex-
tremes have been defined, let them look at people in Ruth's life (not
only people she knows or has known well, but people she knows
professionally and on a casual basis) and see where they fall on
the continuum (mark their place with a cross). It is likely that in
fact people fall all along the continuum, and sometimes people
shift from one position to another at different points in time. For
example, Ruth may place Michael relatively high when she con-
siders how steadfast and supportive he has been, and relatively low
when she feels he has rebuked her or let her down. It may also
become clear that most people are a mixture. Even her brother
influenced her parents to visit her when she was ill. Conversely,
even God is not always there [17]. Once the exercise has been completed, Ruth should be asked again to rate her belief in the statement: 'No-one can be trusted'. Assuming its credibility is reduced,
they can then work to formulate a new assumption which she will
need to test for accuracy and helpfulness on a day-to-day basis by
experimenting with behaving in accordance with it. This is likely to
be expressed in less black and white terms and might be something
like: 'You can trust some of the people some of the time. The trick
is to discover who can be trusted with what and when'. The therapist will need to know (0–100%) how far Ruth believes this new
assumption.

It is important that changes are not left at this abstract verbal
level, but translated into changes in thinking and behaviour on an
everyday basis. These changes can be framed in terms of testing out
the validity of the new assumption outlined above – finding out
through direct experience if it will hold water. Change on a daily
level also means modifying the conditional assumption that trusting people will necessarily lead to hurt or abuse. Again, a continuum
considering what 'trust' means may be helpful:

0 ——————————————————————————————— 100

Do not trust at all   Trust completely

As before, they need first to decide what exactly the two poles mean, and then to work out what 'trust' might mean at different points on the continuum. For example, you might trust a shop assistant to give you the correct change, but would not consider it appropriate to tell her your deepest secrets. You might trust a particular friend with intimate disclosures, but not be able to trust her to be on time. The end point they are aiming for is that trust means different things with different people and under different circumstances. What is appropriate and safe in one situation is not necessarily so in another. A real problem with the 'better safe than sorry' position is that you never learn to make these accurate discriminations, and also that you do not learn to deal with and repair breaches of trust. Once a person lets you down, they go from 100 to 0, and that's it.

2 *Changing immediate reactions: Behavioural experiments*. The final step is to use the re-evaluation of fundamental principles as a basis for cognitive and behavioural changes in specific situations as they arise. The therapist and client need together to set up a sequence of experiments, week by week, when Ruth takes steps towards greater trust and evaluates the results. Experiments need to be carefully recorded, for example by noting: (i) what she predicts will happen if she behaves in a new way and how far (0–100%) she believes the prediction; (ii) the nature of the experiment (what she will actually do to test the prediction); (iii) what the outcome is; (iv) how far she now believes the original prediction; (v) what she has learned from the experiment; and (vi) what she needs to do next. It will be important week by week to examine the effects of these experiments on the degree of belief (0–100%) in the old assumptions and the reformulations which are taking their place. Good experiments should lead to decay in the old system and growth in the new.

The aim is to proceed exactly as Ruth advocates to the young people who attend her assault course; that is, to move step by step at her own pace, acknowledging the risk and going for it when she is ready. It would probably be a good idea for therapist and patient to organize the experiments in terms of a hierarchy of risk, starting with small changes with relatively safe people, and moving in the direction of greater risk as Ruth's confidence grows. In essence, they are building a bridge between the two trees, rather than requiring her to make a dangerous leap into the unknown.

Date	Emotion(s) What do you feel? How bad was it (0–100%)?	Situation What were you doing or thinking about?	Automatic thoughts What exactly were your thoughts? How far did you believe each of them (0–100%)?	Rational response What are your rational answers to the automatic thoughts? How far do you believe each of them (0–100%)?	Outcome 1. How far do you now believe the thoughts (0–100%)? 2. How do you feel? (0–100%)? 3. What can you do now?

Figure 3 Daily record of negative automatic thoughts

3 *Changing immediate reactions: Dealing with negative automatic thoughts*. It is likely that while these changes are taking place, and even when she is well on the way, Ruth will continue to encounter situations that activate the old system and make her feel vulnerable and exposed, or alternatively deprived of comfort or affection. It will be important to monitor these as they occur so that associated negative automatic thoughts can be identified and questioned using guided discovery. This is usually done on a daily record of negative automatic thoughts (see the version shown in Fig. 3).

The steps involved are as follows:

1 Identify the unpleasant emotion that tells you negative thinking is in progress. Rate it for intensity (0–100%).
2 Identify the situation which has triggered the emotion.
3 Identify the negative automatic thoughts associated with the emotion (words, images, implicit meanings). Rate belief in each (0–100%).
4 Question the thoughts: What is the evidence for and against them? What might be a more realistic perspective? What biases or exaggerations are present? How might another person view the situation?, etc. Write down the answers to the questions and rate belief (0–100%) in each.
5 Now go back to the original thoughts and re-rate belief in them. Similarly, re-rate the intensity of the original emotions. If you have found effective answers, these ratings should have fallen.
6 Develop an action plan. How can you test the validity of the alternative thoughts? How can you react differently next time a similar situation arises? What other situations might the new perspective apply to?

To show what I mean, let me take Ruth's thoughts and feelings in the waiting room as an example (this is based on information in the tape and transcript, but necessarily goes beyond it).

Emotions:	Alienated, tearful, uptight, frightened, vulnerable (85%)
Situation:	Waiting to see Michael
Thoughts:	I don't want somebody cold and clinical, I want comfort and warmth (100%). I don't want a man (100%). I can't tell him, it'll make me too vulnerable (95%). I don't want to expose myself to him (100%). If I tell him how I feel, I'll just push him away (95%). I mustn't cry (95%). I won't be able to let go (98%).
Alternatives:	This is an old system operating – it's my fear that closeness will lead to hurt or abuse (100%). Is that

really relevant here? What evidence do I have that Michael is either cold and clinical or abusive? Not a lot (85%). In fact he's stood by me now for 18 months, and seems willing to keep helping me to get where I want to go – fact (100%). It's true he's not perfect – he doesn't always give me what I want (100%). But actually that's a lot to do with making sure he doesn't abuse me or break boundaries (80%).

Re-rate belief
in thoughts: 100%, 90%, 70%, 60%, 55%, 30%, 65%
And emotions: 60%
Action plan: Try being up front with him as an experiment. Observe his reactions closely for evidence of either coldness or abuse.

4 *How therapy may progress.* The interweaving of immediate and long-term change strategies described here is typical of the way cognitive therapy might be used with people whose difficulties are of long standing and have had an enduring and consistent effect on their lives. This has been called 'schema-focused cognitive therapy'. It normally requires a time-frame longer than the 12–20 sessions typically offered for acute difficulties – say eighteen months to two years. Much of the necessary work will already have been done (exploration of issues, building a therapeutic relationship), but Ruth should still anticipate six to eight months of working systematically on the old system in order to achieve lasting change. It may well not be necessary to meet on a weekly basis throughout this period. Weekly sessions are likely to be essential to start with in order to question and reformulate the old beliefs and to initiate a strategy for change, not least because of the degree of danger Ruth will feel. However, once she is clear about what to do and is able to use her new cognitive and behavioural skills effectively, her confidence will grow. They may then wish to meet less frequently, and to use sessions to monitor progress and to deal with the hiccups and setbacks that will inevitably occur. The option of unscheduled 'emergency' meetings at times of particular difficulty could also be retained.

Conclusion

This has been a fascinating experience. I am struck by how far the content of what Michael is doing echoes what one would also be doing in cognitive therapy, and yet how different the style is. As a novice cognitive therapist, he already has much on his side: his ability to form a warm, accepting relationship, his very high level of empathic skill, and his ability to tune into 'hot' issues and to relate them to events in the past and the present (the rudiments of a conceptualization). The areas in which he needs to develop his skills are: developing and sharing a cognitive conceptualization, 'guided discovery' skills, treatment structure, and the systematic use of carefully monitored cognitive and behavioural change procedures.

Now that this discussion of the material is coming to an end, I should like Michael to look back at what I have covered and to ask himself, 'What have I gained from this supervision session?', and to summarize in writing what he thinks the key points are. When he has done so, I would like him to note three specific things that he will take away and use in practice next time he sees Ruth. Finally, let him see if he can find some concrete, specific answers to the following question: 'What do I now need to do in order to develop my cognitive therapy knowledge and skills further?'

Further reading

Beck, A.T. (1976). *Cognitive Therapy and the Emotional Disorders*. New York: International Universities Press. (Also available in Penguin.)

Freeman, A., Pretzer, J., Fleming, B. and Simon, K. (1990). *Clinical Applications of Cognitive Therapy*. New York: Plenum Press.

Hawton, K., Salkovskis, P.M., Kirk, J. and Clark, D.M. (1989). *Cognitive Behaviour Therapy for Psychiatric Problems: A Practical Guide*. Oxford: Oxford Medical Publications.

Jehu, D. (1988). *Beyond Sexual Abuse: Therapy With Women Who Were Childhood Victims*. Chichester: John Wiley.

Padesky, C.A. (1994). Schema change processes in cognitive therapy. *Clinical Psychology and Psychotherapy*, Vol. 1, pp. 267–278.

Young, J. (1990). *Cognitive Therapy for Personality Disorders: A Schema-focussed Approach*. Saratoga: Practitioners Resource Exchange.

DAVID LIVINGSTONE SMITH

COMMUNICATIVE PSYCHOTHERAPY

The supervisor

My training began with a course in neo-Reichian psychotherapy, about which I became very critical and did not complete. I began professional practice as a neo-Reichian, and after several years grew dissatisfied with this approach. Hoping to draw on aspects of other traditions to remedy its defects, I read widely and was ultimately drawn to Freudian psychoanalysis as my work gradually became suffused with Freudian thinking. I came eventually to realize that I was more committed to Freud than to Reich, and I undertook a Masters degree in psychoanalysis which had a strong clinical component. During this period I had the great good fortune to be taught and clinically supervised by some of the most prominent Freudian psychoanalysts in the UK.

It was during my Freudian phase that I first encountered the communicative approach, a theory and method of psychotherapy largely derived from psychoanalysis. Communicative theory claims that human beings are designed to understand one another. Even when consciously occupied with other matters, we silently monitor the behaviour of others. According to communicative theory, there are special circuits in the brain (or, if you prefer, 'parts of the mind') which are *dedicated* to this process. These neural circuits have been evolved over the millennia to enable us to size up our fellow human animals as quickly and accurately as possible. Operating outside of awareness, this neural system is rather poetically referred to as the 'deep unconscious wisdom system' (Langs 1993). The deep unconscious wisdom system is an 'organ for interpersonal perception', which has an indirect impact upon the conscious part of the mind. During those moments when we are sufficiently freed from practical concerns to allow our minds to wander, memories and 'images' seem to emerge spontaneously. According to communicative theory, the deep unconscious wisdom system expresses itself by evoking such thoughts. Thoughts evoked by the activity of the deep unconscious wisdom system are distinguished by being concrete, specific and vivid. When we express these thoughts to others, we usually do so in the form of stories. So when someone tells you a story which has just 'popped into their head', – a story that is not directly concerned with their immediate circumstances – it is likely that you are hearing the voice of the deep unconscious wisdom system. Communicative therapy calls these stories 'derivatives', a term borrowed from Freud.

This process is very easy to study in the context of psychoanalytic psychotherapy, because psychoanalytic patients are encouraged to allow thoughts to pop into their heads and to report them (Freud's 'fundamental rule' of free association). Patients in psychoanalysis and psychoanalytic therapy therefore usually spend a lot of time telling stories.

We can understand the deeper meaning of these stories by wondering what they have to do with the storyteller's immediate situation. Again, this is easy to do in the context of psychotherapy, because it is only the rather limited therapeutic environment (including the therapist) that impinges directly and immediately upon the patient. Communicative psychotherapists therefore regard stories of this type emerging in the context of psychotherapy sessions as *always* related in some way to the therapeutic environment. In order to understand their unconscious meaning, it is necessary to find out just what it is in the therapeutic environment that the patient is responding to (in the communicative jargon, this is called 'identifying the *trigger*'). You also need to identify the themes which the stories express. This is done by concentrating on the actions, relationships and qualities expressed in the stories, and 'mapping' them on to the trigger.

Perhaps an example will clarify this. Imagine that a therapist has made a rather aggressive remark to his patient (the trigger) and that the patient responds by saying, 'I once had a neighbour who beat his wife'. The theme of this remark can be expressed as 'Someone near to me beat someone else instead of caring for her as he should'. Now, when we bring this theme into relation with the trigger we get an explosion of meaning. The patient seems to be saying, 'In intervening as you did, you are committing an act of violence against me instead of caring for me as you should'.

People sometimes misunderstand this approach, and think that communicative therapists rigidly claim that *everything* that patients say is *really* about their therapists. This is false on two counts. In the first place, patients do more than tell stories. Indeed, some rarely if ever tell stories. It is only stories of the kind described above that are said to carry deep unconscious meaning. Second, just because a story carries unconscious meaning does not prevent it from carrying conscious meaning as well. I can use a book to prop open a door, but that does not stop it from being a book. Many true descriptions can be given of any event or situation, but this does not mean that we are free to pick and choose as the spirit moves us. If we are setting out to understand the psychological dynamics at play between patient and therapist, we must address their stories in this spirit. If we have some other aim – for example, to determine the phenomenological dimensions of patients' experiences – there is no reason why we should not use their stories differently.

Mother Nature has designed the deep unconscious wisdom system to function in a stable and reliable manner (although like all biological systems, it will malfunction under certain circumstances). As such, it responds consistently to the stimuli which we encounter. Certain features of the therapeutic environment or 'frame' (as it is called in communicative jargon) will almost always elicit unconscious disapproval. Other features consistently elicit approval. By paying attention to just what features of the therapeutic environment receive unconscious approval, again and again, from one patient to the next, it has been possible to form an idea of the optimal way to structure this type of therapeutic environment. This secured frame includes the following components:

1 A secure and reliable setting in which there is a fixed place, time and duration for each meeting.
2 An appropriate fee to insure that the therapist is employed by and accountable to the patient.
3 Privacy and confidentiality, with no third-party intrusions.
4 A patient-centred therapist who does not permit his or her personal concerns to intrude into the psychotherapeutic work.
5 A therapist who refrains from any form of coercion.
6 A therapist who refrains from physical contact.
7 A therapist who will confine his contact with the patient to the psychotherapeutic hour and who has had no extra-therapeutic relationship with the patient either before, during or after the therapy.

The great consistency of unconscious reactions to the frame allows us to predict that when the frame is modified so as to deviate from these criteria, patients will offer disguised criticisms of their therapists by means of the stories that they tell.

The technique of communicative psychotherapy relies on drawing on patients' unconscious wisdom. Communicative psychotherapists take patients' unconscious commentaries very seriously and attempt to conduct the therapy on the basis of their guidance. Communicative interpretations always refer to the real implications of therapists' actions and omissions. The main task of the communicative supervisor is to help the supervisee 'translate' these unconscious messages and to put them into effect. It follows from this that communicative psychotherapists reject the notion of 'transference' – the idea that patients unconsciously and inappropriately distort their experience of the present in terms of the past. Therapists have to implicate *themselves* when considering what happens in therapy. This turns out to be quite difficult, because the stories that patients tell portray much of what therapists do in a very unfavourable light.

Communicative therapists evaluate their interventions against the touchstone of their patients' unconscious comments. If an intervention is followed by a story with a negative theme, the intervention is regarded as erroneous. An intervention is regarded as correct if and only if the patient responds to it with a positively toned narrative, a phenomenon called 'derivative validation'. It is usually possible to predict accurately what kind of response a given intervention will elicit.

If the deep unconscious wisdom system responds exclusively to proximal stimuli in the therapeutic environment, how does the patient's past enter into the work? It is sensible to assume that patients' histories exert a profound influence upon what happens to them in therapy. Psychotherapists often assume that the past can only enter the present through the medium of explicit (although disguised and unconscious) memories of past events. But this is not the only way to conceptualize matters. Communicative psychotherapists are more inclined to understand the past as preserved implicitly in the *way* that the deep unconscious wisdom system processes information. It seems that early experiences may 'tune' the deep unconscious system so that it is readily able to detect only certain 'wavelengths' of experience. Crucial developmental experiences influence the selectivity of the deep unconscious wisdom system. Generally speaking, the mind recognizes most readily those properties of events to which in the past it has had to adapt. So, for example, an individual who was beaten as a child will be most attuned to the violent aspects of a stimulus, while one who was spoiled will most readily recognize the undermining aspects.

Although the secured frame possesses powerfully constructive properties, it also evokes 'death anxiety' (the dread of one's own mortality). The reason for this is unknown, but it has been suggested that the frame universally symbolizes the boundary between life and death (Langs 1994). The seemingly inevitable mobilization of death anxiety impels both psychotherapists and patients to deviate from the optimal frame, even if these deviations are perceived to be destructive. If the secured frame represents death, modification of the frame represents the transcendence of death. Some patients and therapists who are particularly vulnerable to death anxiety are therefore unable to tolerate an unmodified application of the communicative approach.

Langs' radical reformulation of psychoanalysis excited me, but at the time there were no opportunities in Britain for training in the communicative approach. I had no alternative but to teach myself and, having done this, to establish frameworks for training others. Now, twelve years on, I continue to advocate the communicative approach. My style of practice is quite 'orthodox' and I do not knowingly draw on elements from other approaches, save in cases where the use of the communicative method is clearly inappropriate.

My general view of psychotherapy undoubtedly colours the spirit of my therapeutic and supervisory practice. I believe that the practice of psychotherapy and the theories which inform it are at an extremely primitive level of development. All psychotherapists work in ignorance, although many pretend that this is not the case. I think that one consequence of this is that present-day psychotherapy has great potential for inflicting harm and that psychotherapists need to be alert to the iatrogenic syndromes that may result from their (inevitably) fumbling efforts. I do not think that the communicative approach is the 'last word' in psychotherapy and I assume that the advance of knowledge will one day render it obsolete. In light of this I attempt, not always successfully, to maintain a somewhat sceptical attitude to my own theoretical commitments.

Initial assessment of the session

As a communicative supervisor, I am most concerned to establish how the patient and therapist respond to the emotionally fraught realities of the frame. I will therefore first identify the main respects in which this particular setting deviates from the ideal. Once this is done, I will adhere to the standard communicative practice of using the theory in conjunction with information about the frame to make some predictions about the thematic content of the session. This is standard procedure in communicative supervision, and I make these predictions without yet having read the transcript of the session.

If they turn out to be wide of the mark, this will count against the communicative theory. I will then remark on some of the pertinent clinical material mentioned in Jacobs' introductory account before going on to describe my initial impression of the transcript.

The most outstanding and unusual deviation in this therapeutic relationship is the fact that therapist and patient are involved in a professional collaboration which will severely modify the confidentiality of the treatment. I therefore predict that the patient will tell stories involving exposure, exploitation (the therapist is, in a sense, using the patient to further his career) and third-party intrusions. All of these issues will, I assume, be reinforced by the fact that the session was tape-recorded and that transcripts were to be sent to various third parties.

Another important issue is that the therapist and patient had previously been in a teacher/student relationship, which had also involved the therapist's wife and on at least one occasion included a physical embrace with the patient. I anticipate that this will be unconsciously experienced by the patient as inconsistent as well as somewhat seductive and perverse. I predict that the patient will offer images of inconsistent behaviour or possibly role incompatibility as well as perversion and sexual seduction.

I anticipate that the various other frame-related issues alluded to in the therapist's introduction will be largely overshadowed by these. Also, I anticipate that the therapist's vested interest in the project will make it extremely difficult for him to appreciate the depth of his patient's distress, and I predict that he would be inclined to intervene in a rather defensive manner, that his patient will unconsciously experience him as defensive and remote as well as actively persecutory and that these themes will also be expressed in her narratives. I wonder if the fact of the therapist's vested interest might, in the end, make it difficult for this patient to express her point of view.

Jacobs notes in his introductory remarks that during the week following his proposal to Ruth that they record a session for use in this book, she 'turned down two requests for help made to her by others . . . on the grounds that she felt pressurized by them'. Interpreting this communicatively, I hypothesize that Ruth was unconsciously telling Jacobs that she did not want to comply with his proposal. It is not uncommon for our unconscious views to be at odds with our conscious views, and Ruth's agreement to participate should be understood in this light. Also, during the first tape-recorded session Ruth spoke of her impending operation, linking this to her earlier accident, exposure and rape. I take these themes to portray the implications of the book project and tape-recording.

Turning now to the transcript of the session, my initial impression is that my predictions are largely confirmed. The patient's material contains a good deal of unconscious communication pertaining mainly to the implications of the therapist using the session as the basis for his book. The therapist, who is quite active, does not interpret her stories in light of this trigger and confines himself to the manifest content of her discourse, thus implicitly informing the patient that he has difficulty acknowledging Ruth's unconscious communications and the emotional implications of his own actions. The patient is put in the position of having to come to terms with the persecutory implications of the framework deviation while, at the same time, adapting herself to the therapist's unawareness of the impact of his own behaviour.

At this point I become concerned about how I will be able to express all of this tactfully to the therapist. Although psychotherapists express interpretations to their patients, it is often difficult for them to accept their patients' unconscious interpretations of *them*. This is a difficulty with which communicative supervisors are all too familiar. How can I authentically 'translate' the patient's disguised commentary without traumatizing the supervisee?

Further information on the therapy and the client

I was concerned to establish what other aspects of the therapeutic setting and relationship the patient might be responding to in this session.

The therapist charges the patient less than his usual fee. This may be important, as the patient may feel that on a reduced fee she does not really 'own' the therapy and cannot insist on a secure therapeutic relationship. By the same token, the therapist may feel that this gives him license to use the patient for his book project. I also learned that the RAF Benevolent Fund has paid for some of the sessions, which brings in another third-party involvement. The patient will also be paid for her contribution to the book, which highlights the role ambiguities in this therapy. Although on the conscious level there is no necessary conflict between the editor/contributor and therapist/patient relationships, unconsciously this is usually regarded as violently contradictory. Ruth does not pay for the sessions that she cancels, which is also a deviation from the optimal frame as currently understood by communicative psychotherapists.

Other frame issues likely to adversely affect the patient are that Ruth occasionally meets the therapist's wife in the corridor, that the therapist changes the time of appointments at the patient's request and that, on such occasions, they may meet in a different room. There is a shared waiting area (which is usually, but not always, empty at the time of Ruth's appointments) and a receptionist is present. Although these factors may seem trivial, communicative theory holds that they have significant unconscious ramifications. They further erode the security of the therapeutic relationship and place constraints upon what can be accomplished within it.

Finally, I learned that when Jacobs linked Ruth's concerns about exposure with the tape-recording and the book, four sessions before the present one, he did not attempt to reduce it to a transference fantasy but implicitly affirmed the plausibility of Ruth's perspective. Unfortunately, he does not appear to have treated Ruth's references to sexual abuse in the same way.

Detailed comments on the session

As a communicative supervisor, my primary task is to help supervisees understand and use their patients' unconscious insights. I will therefore refrain from speculation about the significance of Ruth's life history. I have indexed each of my comments to the corresponding sections of the session transcript by means of the numerals in square brackets.

The session begins [1] with Ruth upset and uncertain about attending, implicitly expressing a need for psychotherapeutic help. The therapist's task is to listen carefully to Ruth so as to understand the basis of her distress. If he listens silently, she will probably tell him. Instead of remaining silent, however, the therapist speaks, suggesting to the patient that she cry. This is a non-neutral intervention. Ruth both wishes to weep and to refrain from weeping. In suggesting that she cry, Jacobs takes sides with one side of Ruth's personality over and against another. Like all omissions and commissions, this speaks volumes about the therapist. Jacobs shows that he has some investment in the patient's crying, and wants to ignore or override her reluctance.

Ruth continues with an expression of resistance ('I feel I can't speak to you . . . I just feel alienated') and distress. Sometimes we unconsciously use ourselves to represent others, a process which psychoanalysts call 'introjection'. So Ruth may well be unconsciously saying that she experiences Jacobs as alienated and unable to communicate with her. Again, I advise silence at this juncture. We need to know what is going on in the psychotherapeutic situation which makes it difficult for Ruth to express herself openly. Instead of silently listening, which is what I recommend, Jacobs presses her for more information.

Ruth goes on [3] to describe her resistance. She implies that she no longer trusts her therapist and that she finds it difficult to speak to him. According to communicative theory, resistance is always an interactional phenomenon; it always involves a significant contribution from the therapist. I therefore believe that Jacobs needs to consider his own contribution to the patient's difficulties. He should ask himself what it is that he has done to erode Ruth's trust. In his position, I would first review the possibilities. I would then force myself to remain silent, listening for Ruth's references to triggers.

Ruth does allude to a trigger, mentioning Moira and Barbara, who are third parties to treatment. This suggests that Ruth is distressed and resistant because Jacobs has severely compromised the privacy and confidentiality of her treatment. The most proximal aspect of this trigger is the presence of the tape-recorder. Towards the end of [3] Ruth engages in an episode of unconscious communication when she says that she could attribute her state to the effect of the general anaesthetic. A general anaesthetic is a substance administered to render one unconscious of the pain caused by an invasive medical procedure. Ruth may see the tape-recording (and the book project which lies behind it) as cutting into her personal boundaries and the boundaries of the psychotherapy. She may also feel that the therapist needs to keep her from being aware of this: his interventions may have an 'anaesthetic' quality. Jacobs' intervention is unnecessary and once again has a somewhat non-neutral quality, as he contests her view of the effects of the anaesthetic.

Ruth goes on to talk about her resistance [4], expressing uncertainty about how much of it is due to Jacobs as a man and how much stems from the psychotherapy. This provides a 'bridge to therapy', linking the resistance to the therapeutic situation. Ruth's discourse is becoming more and more clearly related to the frame issues impinging upon her.

Jacobs responds with a lengthy intervention, which introduces material that the patient has not mentioned. Therapists often do this when there is something going on in a session that frightens them. I find this intervention rather confusing. He seems to be saying that Ruth perceives him as 'cold' because of her early experiences with a mother who rejected her. As he mentions the tape-recording in this context, the intervention might, indeed, be seen to possess an 'anaesthetic' quality. It is as though he were saying, 'Let's talk about you and your mother instead of the real implications of what I am doing with you'. Jacobs both presents Ruth's attitude as more sexual than she herself has ('that's red-hot stuff') and *refrains* from interpreting this in terms of her childhood. This reminds me of an anecdote presented by Ralph Greenson (1967) in *The Technique and Practice of Psycho-Analysis*. Greenson wrote of a patient that:

> He had been a life-long Republican . . . and he had tried, in recent months, to adopt a more liberal point of view, because he knew I was so inclined. I asked him how he knew I was a liberal and anti-Republican. He then told me that whenever he said anything favourable about a Republican politician, I always asked for associations. On the other hand, whenever he said something hostile about a Republican, I remained silent, as though in agreement. Whenever he had a kind word for Roosevelt, I said nothing. Whenever he attacked Roosevelt, I would ask who did Roosevelt remind him of, as though I was out to prove that hating Roosevelt was infantile.
>
> (Greenson 1967: 273)

In the present session, Jacobs interprets Ruth's lack of trust in him as something infantile, but offers no interpretations purporting to explain her sexual attraction to him, as though to imply that this attraction is only natural and does not require psychoanalytic explanation. Taken as a whole, this intervention is rather seductive.

Ruth contests Jacobs' portrayal of her attitude towards him [5]. Her reference to feeling 'exposed' may well allude to the book project and the tape-recording. Jacobs responds by attempting to convince her. Even the idiom of this intervention possesses an erotic quality ('the man bit . . . red hot . . . brings up . . . very hard').

As a rule, I think that an interpretation should be offered only once. If the interpretation doesn't 'click', this means that there is something wrong, and that the therapist should silently reconsider his hypothesis. The temptation to repeat an intervention, to justify it or to hammer a point home betrays some urgent personal need within the therapist which is being thrust upon the patient. Jacobs is clearly in a state of intense counter-transference at this point in the session. A period of silent self-analysis is in order.

Tension is building rapidly. The situation has become quite complicated, as the patient must now deal both with the frame issues of the tape-recording, the book project and so on, along with the implications of the therapist's verbal interventions. Ruth again mentions her feeling of being exposed and her reluctance to come to therapy [6]. She then goes on to tell a story describing how she refused a lift from a friend and decided to drive herself because it made her more free. Ruth's story expresses the theme of preferring autonomy to dependence on someone else. This sounds like what communicative psychotherapists call a 'model of rectification', an unconscious recommendation to the therapist. Here, Ruth seems to be saying that she would prefer to terminate therapy (drive herself) than be dependent upon Jacobs. Alternatively, she may be proposing to Jacobs that *he* should sever the ties with third parties.

Jacobs responds with a transference interpretation, claiming that he stands for those who have rejected and sexually attacked Ruth. This is another 'anaesthetic' intervention which implies that Ruth's responses to Jacobs stem from her past experiences. But his management of the frame and his interventions really do have sexually attacking and rejecting properties. There is a clear sense in which he is *really* sexually attacking Ruth (through his interventions) and rejecting her attempts at addressing the vital issues. Without realizing it, he is saying that he will not or cannot own the implications of his own behaviour.

Ruth emphasizes that she does not want to expose herself to Jacobs [7], which is perfectly understandable when considered in light of the foregoing analysis. She mentions the coldness and sterility of the hospital and how these evoke memories of her sexual assault and accident, and in the course of this alludes to a tape-recorder. I understand this as an unconscious comment on the therapeutic situation: 'Your recording of this session for the book, and your manner of intervening, are cold and sterile and remind me of being gang-raped and smashed up'. Although he alludes to the taping, Jacobs does not connect any of this with himself. Now, we know that he was aware of the relationship between these stories and the book project because he has told us in his introductory remarks that these themes made their appearance in the *first* tape-recorded session and that he had interpretatively linked them, a point which will soon become significant.

Ruth next tells a story about her experience in hospital [8]. Although the hospital staff were well-intentioned, the nurse kept coming in to check on her when she needed to sleep. In the past, thoughts of the therapist had enabled her to sleep, but on this occasion Ruth wanted her teddy bear, as there was nobody there to comfort her. The nurse's incessant checking is an apposite image for the therapist's frequent interventions during the session thus far. Ruth feels alone, and seeks something to provide her with the sense of security which the therapist is unable to offer.

Ruth reports a dream in which the therapist features manifestly. Lectures are *public* events: one lectures to an audience. The presence of Jacobs at the lecture may refer to the way that the book project makes public her therapy with him. In the dream, both Jacobs and Brian are in an evaluative role *vis-à-vis* Ruth. It may well be that given the public quality of their work together, Ruth feels under pressure to say only those things of which Jacobs approves. Brian and Jacobs coming to regard Ruth as on the right track may be a model of rectification; that is, a suggestion to Jacobs that he understand and appreciate her unconscious messages about psychotherapy. Ruth does not provide any free associations to the dream, only some rather intellectualized ruminations, so it is not possible to offer anything more than a tentative analysis. The reference to having had physical contact with Brian, and wanting to hug him, may allude to Jacobs having hugged Ruth prior to the start of their therapeutic relationship. Unfortunately, Jacobs takes up and attempts to extend Ruth's ruminations on the dream, continuing this in [10] and bringing in her alleged fear of his sexuality.

Through [11] to [16] Ruth develops a very powerful narrative about her experience in hospital, describing how the anaesthetist told her that when she felt the anaesthetic being injected her consciousness would be obliterated. This suggests that Ruth experiences the therapy – and especially Jacobs' interventions – as something intended to obliterate awareness. We can consider this in two ways. Ruth may experience the interventions as attempting to obliterate her awareness. Alternatively, or simultaneously, she may have unconsciously concluded that Jacobs is attempting to obliterate his own awareness of the significance of his actions, in which case the anaesthetic stands for his own defences.

Prior to the anaesthetic taking effect, the surgeon held her hand and stroked her hair in a way that felt comforting. Communicatively speaking, this is a somewhat puzzling image. I certainly did not expect a positively toned image at this juncture. It is probably best understood as pertaining to Jacobs' linking of the theme of exposure with the appropriate trigger in a prior session. This was before the 'anaesthetic' took effect – that is, before Jacobs had suppressed his understanding of the unconscious significance of Ruth's stories.

The surgery (therapy) is described as an intrusive procedure during which she was stripped naked. The reference to the heart monitor may relate to the presence of the tape-recorder. Ruth emphasizes that she had expected to be covered rather than exposed, and that the exposure was emotionally hurtful and made her feel 'cold' and 'interfered with'. She wanted to withdraw. I take this to mean that, deep down, Ruth feels violated and exposed by the circumstances of this psychotherapy. The wish to withdraw sounds like the expression of an unconscious wish to terminate the therapy. Jacobs does not respond to these unconscious dimensions of the material and, especially in [11], introduces his own associations about 'leering' and 'visual rape'. Ruth has not mentioned leering and visual rape, so the introduction of these themes may express Jacobs' personal concerns. It may be that he unconsciously experiences his own use of Ruth as violently and voyeuristically erotic.

In [14] Ruth discusses the public quality of the operation, a theme that clearly bridges over to the therapeutic situation. Her statement, 'I have no idea how many there are in an operating theatre, but it is almost as if it wasn't Jim who is the surgeon, it was everybody else who was there', eloquently expresses the view that the making public of the therapy destroys her relationship with the therapist. Next, she links the experience of surgery with her earlier experience of sexual abuse, which suggests that she unconsciously regards the therapy as reminiscent of being raped by a gang (a poignant image of the 'supervisors').

Ruth's remarks – 'I don't know whether you can do anything with that' and 'Silly, isn't it?' – sound like requests for an intervention. A good intervention linking her stories to the therapeutic situation is indeed possible at this point, and should be developed along the following lines:

> You've just asked me whether I can do anything with what you have been saying, suggesting that you feel that it has some deeper meaning. You have mentioned me, and the therapy, on several occasions today. You have even mentioned a tape-recorder, like the one running here. You have also spoken a great deal about unpleasant experiences and relationships. You have spoken about being rejected, violated, judged and exposed. When you described your dream, you mentioned giving a lecture – speaking to an audience – and later you spoke of being undressed and exposed to the gaze of all of the people in the operating theatre. This reminded you of being hurt in the accident and being raped by the gang of your brother's friends. The surgeon first comforted you but then subjected you to this. You have also mentioned several times that you have lost trust in me, that you were reluctant to come here and that it is difficult for you to 'expose' yourself to me. You have also been quite upset, and have had problems finding the inner security to fall asleep. I think that all of this may be connected. I think that you may feel, deep down, that in recording of the session for a book and exposing what you bring here to a group of supervisors and a large number of readers I am turning what should be a private process into something public – like a lecture or an operating theatre in which you are stripped and exposed to lots of other people. It sounds like my recording of the session, and

using it for the book, feels like being gang-raped all over again. I am like the surgeon, who subjects you to all of this exposure. Perhaps this is what's making it difficult for you to 'expose' yourself to me and why you were reluctant to come here today. Perhaps what I have been doing to you here has made your experience of the operation just that much more complicated. It's caused you distress and made it difficult for you to sleep. Early on in the session you mentioned that you turned down a lift, preferring to drive here yourself because it made you freer. Later on, you mentioned how an awareness of being exposed made you want to withdraw. Perhaps you are also saying by this that under these circumstances you don't want to have to rely on me any more, that you want to stop therapy and be free of all this, that you are exposed and want to withdraw.

This section [14] is a crucial moment in this session. Ruth offers a very powerful set of coalescing derivatives expressing her raw perceptions of Jacobs' mismanagement of the frame. Taken in conjunction with her expressions of resistance and distress as well as her allusions to the therapeutic situation, Jacobs is offered a special opportunity to intervene in a manner highlighting the persecutory implications of his relationship with Ruth. He does intervene, but does not relate the material to the actualities of the therapeutic situation. Instead, he attributes Ruth's resistance to the re-activation of memories of her traumatic accident and rape. In the light of my analysis of the situation, his intervention has an extremely cold, distancing quality. It is as though he says, 'I don't want to know about my role in your distress'. The intervention completely ignores the real drama of their encounter.

It is hardly surprising that at [15] Ruth next finds herself talking about her surgeon's disturbing coldness and formality, and how she could not square this with the fleeting warmth he had shown her just prior to the operation. The account of the surgeon's strange alternation between modes of relatedness may well pertain to Jacobs' contradictory interventions. Ruth knows that he knows that the themes which she has just expressed pertain to the tape-recording and the book project. Why, then, does he now hang everything on Ruth's past experiences and leave himself out of the picture? Indeed, if he understands these matters, why doesn't he turn off the tape-recorder and abandon the book project? Ruth rightly notes – unconsciously – that Jacobs is behaving inconsistently. Ruth's comment about the surgeon treating her coldly when she was *compos mentis* may refer to his unresponsiveness to her incisive unconscious comments and his inclination to interpret this material as expressing her confusion and infantilism. He next offers a lengthy interpretation to the effect that Ruth's feelings have to do with a fear of her own intense longings to regress to a condition of infantile dependence.

Ruth contests Jacobs' interpretation [16], emphasizing that she is frightened of being dominated and undermined. He concurs with this, again without relating it to the relationship existing between them.

Ruth mentions her need to protect herself from her therapist ('my feeling of . . . pushing you away now') [17]. After a few ruminations about Brian, Ruth offers a very moving commentary on the therapy:

> . . . I presume God was looking down on me the last couple of days, but I wondered where the hell He was at times . . . I wish he would take me in his arms and hold me . . . Will I ever be able to have that trust again, as a child? [17]

I take this as a desperate and impassioned plea for a secure holding environment. Ruth no longer trusts her therapist to provide this, and is uncertain whether this trust can ever be restored. The description of God observing her but not intervening sounds like a portrayal of Jacobs' failure to respond to her urgent concerns. She goes on to mention Jacobs, providing a bridge to therapy, and thereby giving him a second opportunity to address these vital issues. Once again, he hangs all of Ruth's difficulties on her past experiences without implicating himself in any way.

Ruth expresses her distress [18], alludes to her resistance, mentions the trigger of third parties (Moira) and refers to not wanting to be exposed. This contrasts sharply with the *conscious* idealization of the therapist expressed towards the end of this passage. Long ago, Fairbairn suggested that we tend to deny the persecutory and seductive aspects of those upon whom we depend. This is certainly true of psychotherapy patients, who often consciously idealize their therapists while unconsciously criticizing them. Once again, Jacobs does not relate Ruth's concerns to the traumatic features of their therapeutic relationship.

Ruth returns to the theme of exposure [19], and then goes on to express her sense of being in a double bind ('how can you be angry at somebody who's doing their best for you and keeping you alive?'). How can Ruth reconcile the fact that Jacobs is her therapist with the fact that he is re-traumatizing her? She compares this with her experience of childhood rape ('I got more than I bargained for'). Jacobs interprets what I consider to be a real, *objective* contradiction in the therapeutic situation as a *subjective* contradiction in Ruth's inner world.

The main theme in the account of the assault course [20–22]

seems to be the need to move on, even though the transition may be frightening. This may portray a wish to terminate therapy. Ruth's own comments have a rather intellectualized quality as she struggles to convince herself that she should trust other people. Ruth speaks of telling her charges that she has only crossed the difficult part of the assault course once, and that she did not like it. Earlier, Ruth claimed that she had *never* been on this part of the assault course. So, she depicts a situation in which someone uses dishonesty to motivate others, remarking that this may not be good for leadership. As a comment on the therapy, Ruth seems to be saying that Jacobs is attempting to influence her through dishonest means and that he is trying to get her to do something that he himself is unwilling to do. The theme of dishonesty makes sense in relation to Jacobs' interventions, which make no reference to his own impact upon Ruth. The other theme makes sense in that Ruth may experience Jacobs as demanding that she face painful truths while avoiding painful truths himself. Jacobs then claims that all of Ruth's feelings have been transferred from other situations and that she can express them to him because she *trusts* him. I think that he is offering Ruth a defence. He is inviting her to idealize him in order to seal over her painful, chaotic and persecutory impressions of him.

Ruth's remark [23] that 'if it isn't transferred in here ... you wouldn't have a job to do' might express something about the therapist's professional identity: 'You have to regard this as transference, because if you saw it as a reflection of what's really going on between us you would be unable to regard yourself as a therapist'. Jacobs acknowledges that Ruth feels unsafe, but is silent about how this may be justified in light of his management of the therapeutic environment.

Letting the session run over time, giving Ruth the tape and altering the date of a session are all further modifications of the frame. It is worth noting here that the more a therapeutic environment deviates from the optimum, the easier it becomes to deviate further. Under such circumstances, particularly when there has been no interpretation of unconscious communication, both patients and therapists are inclined to express themselves unreflectively through action (psychoanalysts call this 'acting-out'). Jacobs' extension of the session is one example of this, as is Ruth's request for a hug and Jacobs' compliance with it. On Ruth's side, the request for a hug may express her need for a secure 'holding' environment or a manic denial of the problems existing between the two of them. Jacobs' compliance may stem from an obscure sense that he owes Ruth something, from a manic desire to merge with her or from his sexual counter-transference feelings. I think that the appropriate intervention in such circumstances is to say something like, 'We can talk about that next time'.

Conclusion

Because communicative theory allows us to make predictions, it is a common practice to try and anticipate something of the next session. In this case, I anticipate much of the same. I expect that Ruth will continue to produce stories illustrating the violent and exposing qualities of the book project. In addition to this, Jacobs' extension of the session and compliance with her request for a hug will be experienced as strongly seductive and I anticipate explicitly sexual narratives in the next session.

In my opinion, the best possible outcome for this therapy is termination at the patient's unconscious behest. The therapist should force himself to remain silent, while listening carefully for narrative portrayals of the book project and its implications for therapy. He should be particularly alert to any models of rectification recommending termination. He should interpret this material along the lines suggested in the model interpretation given in the preceding section. It is a mistake to consider this sort of outcome as purely negative. For a therapist in this position to overcome his own counter-transference needs, sufficiently to be able to hear, interpret and act upon his patient's unconscious call for termination, is a very difficult and deeply compassionate achievement. Were Jacobs to do this, he would leave Ruth with a 'positive introject' – a powerful and constructive relational experience – which may have significant therapeutic ramifications.

The proposal that I contribute to this book placed me in a moral dilemma. Once I had signed the contract, I was not at all sure that I had made the right decision. Of course, I think that it is admirable for a psychotherapist to so openly expose his work to supervisory scrutiny. Psychotherapy cannot advance in the absence of published data of this kind.

Jacobs cannot be blamed for failing to attend to Ruth's unconscious messages, as psychoanalytic therapists are not normally taught how to interpret stories in light of their triggers. Like most psychoanalytic therapists, he was probably subjected to psychoanalytic treatment himself. Although I cannot know for sure, I strongly suspect that most psychoanalytic trainees are given analytic 'treatment' which they unconsciously feel to be violent, exploitative and perverse. I imagine that Jacobs' analyst tried to convince him that the disturbing thoughts which popped into his head while free associating were products of his inner world and his infantile past and had little or nothing to do with what was really taking place between them. It seems to be that the established methods of psychoanalytic training ensure that blind-spots are passed down from one generation to the next, sometimes with tragic consequences.

Ruth, too, has shown great courage and generosity in allowing her therapy to be used in this way. However, what is good for research is not necessarily good for Ruth. After all, I think that Ruth experiences me as one of the gang of rapists mentioned in the transcript, and I think that she is justified in doing so. I reasoned that if I refused to contribute, then someone else would take my place and that such a person would in all probability be uninterested in, or unable to translate, Ruth's unconscious messages. Thinking about this, my mind is drawn back to Ruth's dream – the dream in which she is lecturing on psychodynamics [9]. Perhaps Ruth agreed to this project because, deep down, she wanted to teach people what psychotherapy is really about. If so, I hope I have been able to be of some assistance to her and that this compensates in some small measure for my participation in the violation of her psychotherapy.

Further reading

Greenson, R. (1967). *The Technique and Practice of Psycho-Analysis.* London: Hogarth Press.

Langs, R. (1992). *Science, Systems and Psychoanalysis.* London: Karnac.

Langs, R. (1993). *Clinical Workbooks for Psychotherapists.* London: Karnac.

Langs, R. (1994). *Empowered Psychotherapy.* London: Karnac.

Raney, J. (ed.) (1984). *Listening and Interpreting: The Challenge of the Work of Robert Langs.* New York: Jason Aronson.

Smith, D.L. (1991). *Hidden Conversations: An Introduction to Communicative Psychoanalysis.* London: Routledge.

8

SUE WALROND-SKINNER

FAMILY THERAPY

The supervisor

My professional background was initially in social work, most recently in theology, leading to ordination as a priest, but chiefly in family and marital therapy. I completed my training as a social worker in 1970, and after a short period of generic practice, I went to the United States to train as a family therapist at the Ackerman Family Institute, New York.

My own approach is firmly systemic in the sense that I adhere to the 'classic' doctrine of the family group as a whole having a dynamic meaning over and above the sum of its parts. I believe that the behavioural, cognitive and emotional worlds of the individual can only be understood properly within the context of his or her family system.

This is therefore my starting point for trying to understand Ruth, and the therapist's approach to helping her. Moreover, in common with most family therapists, I conceive of the therapeutic task as being both about understanding and change, and the supervisory task as needing to facilitate the therapist in his efforts to understand the client and help her to change. Again, I conceive of 'change' as involving cognitive, emotional and behavioural change. I would not normally feel comfortable about the occurrence of behavioural change in the absence of any cognitive or emotional change, but nor would I feel satisfied with the acquisition of greater insight into the meaning of the client's situation, personality, etc., unless this resulted in changes in her life as a family member and, where relevant, in other areas of the client's life.

The goals of family therapy are generally directed towards making changes within the family system which result in shifts in the understanding, experience and behaviour of all its members. This is likely to involve the therapist/counsellor in adopting a range of interventions, which may include interpretations of family system dynamics, the setting of behavioural tasks (either inside the session, between sessions or both) and an engagement between the therapist's 'self' and that of the family members, both in terms of a 'real' relationship and within the transference.

Both in my therapeutic and my supervisory work, I begin by forming hypotheses about the client's/therapist's needs, informed by the theoretical orientation outlined above, and guided by my first impressions of the material, continually revised by the response which my interventions have upon the therapeutic/supervisory situation. Thus, the therapeutic/supervisory situation is, for me, essentially a dynamic engagement with the material in which I am involved, alongside the family/therapist, in a continuous piece of experimental work.

Therefore I at first felt severely limited by the fact that this is an individual client not a family, and by the linear and undynamic nature of this enterprise, which made it feel more like guesswork in the dark! The supervisory process for a family therapist normally takes place in *in vivo*, making use of a number of different methods of live supervision: for example, live supervision without a screen where the supervisor sits in the room but outside the therapeutic process; live supervision using a one-way screen and engaging with the therapist via a telephone link; the 'reflecting screen' whereby supervisor and therapist/family exchange places and engage in some dialogue about the process as it unfolds. The experience of commenting upon a session after the event is therefore somewhat foreign to me.

Initial assessment of the session

So I approached this material as a family therapist and from a family systems perspective. As I read and re-read the transcript, I felt the enormity of the gulf between my own work as a therapist and supervisor of family therapists and the material presented. Feelings of uncertainty and panic arose in me! I felt the impertinence of engaging with the material. What can I offer in this situation? I can appreciate the skill and coherence of the therapeutic work in front of me, but the model, method, ideology and therapeutic base are far from where I am.

I wondered if there were any links to be found, any reflections that could be discovered from other areas of my work, and if so, what those links and reflections might be, which might then increase my confidence in setting about the task. I considered the following:

1 Ruth is an adult survivor of child sexual abuse – I have some experience of this syndrome as a consultant and as a counsellor.
2 Ruth is a trainee counsellor – I have some experience of consulting, supervising and training counsellors, particularly in helping them develop relationship skills, develop professional boundaries around their work and consider issues around the transference.
3 Ruth is a member of a family who has asked for help – I have some experience of working with one family member alone on the dynamics of their family system.
4 Ruth is a practising Christian (and the therapist worked once as a priest) – as a priest I share with her and him a belief system and language.

Nevertheless, it is a challenge to be asked to supervise a piece of work with an individual counsellee from within my own theoretical orientation as a family therapist. It feels like imposing my ideas and concepts instead of listening and enabling and working within the other person's framework.

I find myself very preoccupied with how to convey fully the respect with which I have received this piece of work, and my admiration for its quality, while at the same time offering some different kinds of ideas. Because of this, this supervisory process initially feels to me to be inherently intrusive and abusive, because I am 'entering' the therapeutic process about two years into its life, from a position of ignorance and from a different orientation to therapy.

I wonder how the therapist and the client can be protected from this intrusion? I wonder whether the therapist will be able to benefit from the insights of another, who comes from a different orientation, allowing them to enrich and expand his own approach while remaining true to his own? I wonder whether I may be in danger of naming what may feel for the present to be unnameable for Ruth – and, out of my ignorance of all that has occurred so far, make suggestions that feel inappropriate and premature or, alternatively, useless and already fully considered? I trust that the act of naming some of these potential pitfalls may serve in some way to help them to be avoided.

Questions put to the therapist

In my few questions to Michael:

1 I sought to clarify the nature of the exercise.
2 I sought to discover the kind of work that had already been tackled, particularly concerning the relationship between Ruth and other

members of her family. I asked whether Michael had done any work with Ruth on her family of origin by (a) using a genogram, (b) coaching her in her relationship with family members, or (c) involving other members of the family in therapy. Michael talked of the frequency with which Ruth's mother comes up in the sessions. He said he had not done a genogram, although he often does in his private notes, that he had not coached her in the sense that I meant, and had not involved other family members in a direct way in the therapy.

3 I sought to find out more about the main themes already explored. These included themes of loss and the post-traumatic reactions to stress: loss of a good relationship with parents, of the opportunities of young adult life, and now of her substitute family, the RAF, had been quite fully explored.

4 I sought to discover more about the nature of the transference. I said that I felt it as being more sexual than maternal, but Michael felt that it was crucially and ambivalently both.

5 I sought to clarify Ruth's knowledge of Michael and their shared faith commitment. Michael said that Ruth knows he is a priest.

6 I sought to find out the extent to which I should discuss theory. We clarified that it would be helpful if I discussed: (a) my theoretical orientation as a family therapist, (b) my understanding of the supervisory process as it relates to family therapy, and (c) the connections and areas of difference between both and the current piece of work being offered for supervision.

I therefore begin my detailed comments on the session by a more expanded overview of family therapy theory and family therapy supervision practice.

Detailed comments on the session

I approach this material from the standpoint of a family therapist. Family therapy is a therapeutic intervention which is directed towards the family group as a whole and not towards the individual patient or client. It developed as a therapeutic approach after the Second World War in the United States. By the early 1970s, it had gained a firm identity of its own, distinguished by the seminal work of Gregory Bateson and the communication theorists on the West Coast, by its adaptation of general systems theory to the dynamics of the family, and by its creative extrapolation of some of the more relationally fertile insights of psychodynamic theory to the family group as a whole.

During the last twenty-five years, in which I have practised and taught as a family therapist, there has been an enormous period of flourishing and development in theory, practice and research in the family therapy field, in America, Europe and Britain. There has been a continuous re-working of the early radical insights of family therapy which might be summarized, in a nutshell, as being the belief that it is the family, not the individual, who is the patient or client and which must therefore be the primary focus of therapeutic concern.

Developments in theory have included a polarizing and distinguishing out of approaches between, on the one hand, communicational/strategic and behavioural methods (e.g. the 'Milan' approach, the strategic and brief therapy models of MRI), and on the other, structural, psychodynamic, experiential and object relations approaches (e.g. the Philadelphia School, the Tavistock Clinic, England, and some more person-centred and theme-centred work which emphasizes the symbolic meaning of myths and patterns discernible over several generations of family functioning). There has also been a continuous re-alignment of ideas, which has produced some eclecticism and much revisionism of the harder, harsher lines of demarcation that existed in the 1980s. In particular, constructionism versus realism is an important feature of the post-modern family therapy debate in the 1990s.

The theoretical insights of family therapy which highlight the immediate *in vivo* current interaction between family members within the session and between the therapist and the family, has been progressively mirrored in approaches to supervision. Looking at the therapist's material, after the event, has never seemed to be very congruent with the main thrust of the theoretical orientation. Thus, at an early stage in the development of family therapy, 'live supervision' was introduced.

During the course of putting my questions to Michael, it became progressively clearer that this particular supervisory experience, which at first seemed so different and alien to my usual practice, in fact was much closer than I at first realized. Michael's words, 'Ruth will be looking at the comments you make', began to take on a very powerful, orienting framework for my thinking. Not only was this exercise very close to the practice of live supervision, it actually provided the opportunity for an almost exact replication of a particular model of live supervision, which has been developed by family therapists quite recently. Almost, but not quite! The model of live supervision to which I refer is called the 'Reflecting Team'. It involves the use of a team working behind a one-way viewing screen who, during the course of a session, are invited to make their comments on the therapy as it has progressed so far. While they are doing so, the family, together with the interviewer, watch and listen to the team discussion. In other words, the roles of observer and observed are reversed. The interviewer then discusses with the family their observations on what the team have said. The process can of course be repeated again during the course of the session and it allows for a developing dynamic interchange between the wider therapeutic system of family plus therapist plus supervisory group. It is obviously a logical extension of family therapy theory. In understanding my part in the supervision of Michael in his work with Ruth, I am helped by understanding that there is indeed some dynamic engagement between myself and the 'live' situation of Michael's and Ruth's relationship. The words 'Ruth will be looking at the comments you make' helps me to consider those comments in the light of their subsequent relationship. My comments are affected by the fact that Ruth will read them and this in turn affects my relationship with the supervisee and with the material he has offered to me for supervision.

The supervision session

First, Michael gives the reason for bringing this particular session for supervision as being because Ruth herself saw it as a very important session – and in fact she asked to take a copy of the tape away. Second, the session contains an important theme, which relates to the meaning of physical contact between the therapist and the client – and the way in which this is perceived by each of them.

Michael says that 'the question of such physical contact remains a puzzling one' for him, so that this session is obviously important in highlighting an aspect of the work which poses him with a challenge and a dilemma. This may, I suspect, resonate for him as it does for many of us, on several levels of therapeutic involvement simultaneously: personal, professional and theoretical. I would like to begin by addressing this dilemma on the level of theory, because I think that it helpfully illustrates some of the methodological issues that lie at the heart of the work with Ruth. What is the meaning of the relationship between therapist and client and what role does the therapist play in the client's life during the period of the therapeutic contact, and indeed in some progressively diminishing way afterwards?

As we know from the perspective of psychoanalytic therapy and counselling, the main function of the relationship is to enable a transference to develop with an attendant counter-transference in terms of the therapist's perceptions of the transference, and his own response to it and to the client from his own real feelings. Through this transferential relationship, the client will be able to work through some of the difficulties she has experienced in previous, and especially earlier relationships. In this approach, then, the therapist is a 'transference figure' for the client. Alternatively, from the perspective of various client-centred and humanistic approaches, the relationship becomes a corrective emotional experience through which the client can be healed of some of the privations and/or deprivations she has experienced in other, and especially earlier relationships. The therapist becomes a 'substitutory figure', providing the client with a new, healing and restorative relationship. Yet again, from the perspective of personal construct theory, cognitive and behavioural approaches, the relationship provides the opportunity to explore and try things out in relation to important relationships in the past, or prospective relationships in the future, both relating to the client's real life situation. The therapist becomes a 'coach' or 'guide' in aiding the client's exploration, actions and reflections upon them in the outside world.

This is not of course to suggest that these approaches are going to be strictly 'either . . . or'. They often merge in practice, and this may be one of the therapeutic dilemmas. When is the therapist adopting a usefully eclectic approach and when is he being pushed to behave in ways which are not true to his main orientation and not conducive to the client's well-being? How can boundaries be maintained between methods which are identifiable yet permeable, consistent yet not rigid? The function of every method of counselling and psychotherapy is, at some level, to attend to this very same dilemma that is inherent in the exercise itself – the boundaries between the client and the therapist. All methods of therapy and counselling are intent upon addressing this issue in some measure, so that the curious exercise of the therapeutic experience – cold and clinical in its abstinence, yet warmly and humanely offering so much that is longed for and uniquely given in the therapeutic hour – can be as whole-making, growth-promoting and non-collusive as possible, to the benefit of the client and to the fulfilment of the therapist's own need to be effective.

I was very struck by this boundary question when reading the transcript and listening to the tape. The infringement of real life boundaries and the sexual abuse that followed is a key issue which Ruth is bringing to Michael. This boundary issue is experienced in a critical way by him, and it also reflects my own dilemma, invited to contribute a chapter to a book, but to do so as the supervisor, called in to supervise an actual session, with a real client and a real therapist. Even though I know that this session has occurred sometime in the past, and much will have happened since then, I am also very aware of the parameters and guidelines given to me for this exercise in which I have agreed to take part. I know for example as I have already commented, that my reflections are going to be seen by both the therapist and by the client. As I read and listen therefore, I am drawn into a relationship with them both, but one of a rather peculiar kind, for I shall never meet Ruth and will probably never know how she receives what I say. I am conscious of the burden of responsibility of the exercise. It is one thing to make comments to the therapist within the privacy of the supervisor–therapist relationship, which he can then mull over and process within himself, using what he finds helpful and disregarding the rest. It is quite another to be communicating, in a unilateral way, with the therapist and the client and with the real life client–therapist system. It is not, as I commented earlier, entirely analogous to the live supervision situation, because there is no comeback from Ruth or Michael to me, and no opportunity to introduce that kind of self-corrective mechanism which comes from Michael's or Ruth's response to what I have to say. This poses for me as the supervisor a question about boundaries, somewhat analogous to that which confronts Michael as the therapist. I must be simultaneously aware that my supervisory 'contract' is with him, but that my relationship is in some measure with both him and with Ruth. My interventions must both resist and acknowledge the 'seduction' of a real relationship with Ruth.

In a similar way, there is a three-fold mirroring of the issue of exposure. Exposure, like boundary keeping, is a core theme as I perceive it in this piece of therapeutic work. Ruth has been exposed to the intrusive gaze of others – during her abuse, after her accident and during her hospital treatment. Michael is obviously concerned that the present exercise of exposing her private communications made to him to the public gaze of a group of supervisors, and ultimately to the professional world, should not compound her sense of being exposed without her consent. He too is having to expose his own work to the view of others; and those of us who have been invited to participate must also expose ourselves by 'going into print' and laying ourselves open to the perhaps critical and attacking gaze of others.

The exposure of therapy is always mirrored by the necessary exposure of supervision and, in this case, the further level of exposure of the supervision itself. We are all involved in the dilemma of how and how much to expose ourselves (open ourselves, give of ourselves and thus make ourselves vulnerable) in order to get the help we need, in order to engage with the task before us – of professional and personal development. Thus, both in terms of boundary issues and in terms of the theme of exposure, this exercise is a reflexive one.

But there is also a progression in the therapeutic process and I suspect that this exercise, of engaging with a number of therapists and working with them to bring a book to birth, has come at an important moment in the therapy. The moment is not accidental. Ruth [22] has reached a turning point: 'I want to go over that gap. I don't want to go back'.

Much has been achieved already. Trust has been developed and many profound insights have been gained. Connections have been made between current traumatic experiences and their meaning which comes from the past. Much has been achieved by Ruth in her relationship with Michael and in the work they have done together.

Now perhaps is the moment to move on and to consider how to attend to Ruth's ambivalence about being both a child and an adult, about being dependent and interdependent, being intimate and separate, being in control yet being able to lose herself in love. All these themes, which have been at the heart of the work during the past two years, could perhaps now be worked on more directly in relation to Ruth and her family – and in particular between Ruth and her mother.

Genogram

My first suggestion is therefore to draw up a genogram with Ruth. A genogram is a three-generational map of the relationships and positions of family members within the family system. From the transcript, the bare factual information this would provide would look something like that shown in Fig. 4.

We know that Ruth lives with her parents, and that Stephen lives separately with his wife and child. When that part of the family visits, Ruth is turned out of her room. We know that the relationship between Ruth and Stephen is strained, though she is very fond of her nephew, Jeremy, and by inference her sister-in-law. But most centrally, we know that a huge gulf exists between Ruth and her parents and especially between Ruth and her mother. I suggest that Ruth's teddy bear, which was put up in the attic by her mother, symbolizes the arrested relationship between Ruth and her mother 'put up in the attic' since the time of Ruth's abuse (and, of course, maybe before). At least since Ruth was abused by a group of Stephen's friends at the age of eight. There has I imagine been an enormous gulf between mother and daughter. Her mother seemed to be unable to handle the situation, comfort Ruth or enable her to talk about it,

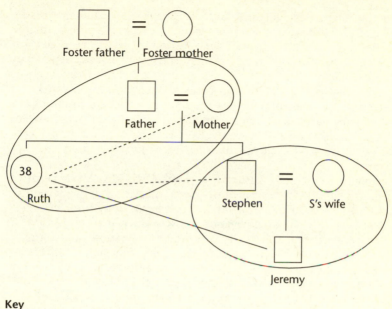

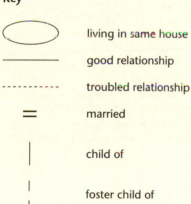

Key

⬭	living in same house
⎯⎯⎯⎯	good relationship
- - - - - -	troubled relationship
=	married
|	child of
¦	foster child of

Figure 4 Ruth's genogram

let alone bring the perpetrators to book. My guess is (and I do my guessing with the utmost tentativeness) there has been anger and disappointment, hurt and longing on Ruth's part; and guilt, shame, anger and perhaps depression in her mother. I believe that the loving, caressing intimacy that Ruth longs for is rooted in the deprivation she feels of a loving intimate relationship with her mother. Of course, such a relationship requires, initially, the total dependency of the helpless, naked baby – quite out of control, entirely at the mercy of her mother's care. Much of what Ruth fears in intimacy seems to me to have its roots in the fear of this early, naked, dependent intimacy.

But because the relationship between Ruth and her mother was arrested at the time of the abuse (and maybe before), it has not been possible for Ruth to experience any progression in this relationship, when she might have been able to experience intimacy and care in an 'inter-dependent' relationship between adult child and her parent.

I say 'maybe before' – because it perhaps has never been possible for Ruth's mother to establish the close intimacy that every mother and baby need to establish. And if this is so, Ruth must grieve at some deep level for the privation as well as for the deprivation of such necessities. If this is the case, there is a serious and difficult question to be asked as to how far Ruth's mother is capable of establishing something warmer and more intimate with Ruth now? I want, however, to start with the premise that there may be some, even if quite limited possibility of doing this; and even if it is a limited relationship and not an ideal one, it would nevertheless be an enormously important step to encourage Ruth to work on it. My major area of hope is that we know nothing of her mother's relationship with *her* parents. We know that her father was brought up by foster parents, but we know nothing about her mother. What I wonder have been *her* areas of sadness and trial, deprivation, privation, loss and hurt? Was she *also*, I wonder, abused as a child? We know that abuse is transmitted through the female line and so I would hypothesize that Ruth's mother has suffered some fundamental abuse in her own childhood. If this is so (and it has of course to be tested), what possibility is there for building the beginnings of empathy and trust between adult mother and child around these shared traumatic experiences?

In working with her on her genogram, it would I think be possible for Michael to elicit from Ruth further important material about the family relationships to add to what he already knows. The purpose of course is to help Ruth reconstruct her family system and her place in it with a view to helping her think about the next steps she might take in working upon some of these relationships now, as they are in the present, and in terms of the way in which they form part of Ruth's current experience now.

We have limited data about them at the moment. But we do know that Ruth's own movements within the system, building upon the insights she has already gained through her work with Michael, and using the supportive strength of her trustful relationship with him, will have a systemic effect upon every relationship within the family. In adopting a family therapy approach, albeit through working with one member of the family only, he will move the therapeutic emphasis towards changing the emotional meaning of current relationships (which will in turn affect the way they are reconstructed in the past) instead of working on the past in order to liberate Ruth to become different in the present.

I suggest, therefore, that Michael works on her genogram during the next two or three sessions with this first goal in mind. The rationale for doing so needs to be talked through with Ruth, in such a way that it forms a continuity with all the work already done, but also introduces a change of direction. Thus the purpose of the genogram should be seen as consolidating the insights already gained; clarifying (as much for him as for her) areas of ignorance and pin-pointing windows of opportunity for bringing about change.

The justification for approaching the issues in this way is three-fold:

1 Ruth is ready to move on – to 'jump the gap'.
2 She lives with her parents, so that her current family is her birth family, and those relationships are very alive and available to be worked with, as well as being currently problematic. The family can therefore be both the unit for and of therapeutic change.
3 It feels as though it is hard for Ruth to take the step towards a fuller mature adulthood in terms of being able 'to work and to love' while she is living in what feels to be a stage of arrested development within her birth family. Working on these relation-ships may free her to move on.

Some useful areas of information to elicit would be:

1 The ages of Ruth's parents.
2 Membership of her father's family. I imagine that her father may have had some foster siblings but may have no blood relatives of whom he is aware. Or is that so? Either way, who were the important people in his upbringing and what does he feel about these experiences? What is his 'story'?
3 Mother's family: What does it consist of? Who is mother still in touch with? Who was she closest to and why – as a child, as an adult? When did important deaths occur? How did she feel about them and how do they connect with each other and with other important emotional events? What is her place in the birth order of her siblings? What is her 'story'?
4 Where did/do family members live in relation to each other? Does

geographical distance/closeness say anything about the emotional closeness or cut-offs between family members?

5 Who is the focus of communications within the family?
6 What have been the major traumatic events in the family?
7 Which relationships are/have been in greatest conflict and which of these remain unresolved?

After this more general mapping of the system, it would be helpful to focus back on Ruth's particular experiences using the following kinds of questions and filling in the answers on the genogram with a brief note of explanation or a line (broken or unbroken) to signify closeness, distance or conflict respectively in the relationships between family members:

1 Does Ruth feel she carries any particular role in the family (e.g. scapegoat, family healer, etc.)?
2 If so, is there anyone else, in another generation perhaps, that she has heard about who carries a similar role?
3 Is there anyone in the family she is said to be like (e.g. is she named after anyone in the family)?
4 To whom does she feel closest?
5 Who does she feel most distant from or in conflict with?
6 Has this changed over the years?
7 Which of the children (Stephen and Ruth) are each of the parents closest to?
8 Which relationship between herself and another family member does she feel to be least satisfactory?
9 What kind of change would she like to achieve in this relationship?

Coaching

The second piece of work may now be possible, that of coaching Ruth in her relationship with her mother. I assume that given all the work Michael has already done, he could complete Ruth's genogram along the above lines within a couple of sessions. It may be that Ruth gives a somewhat peripheral relationship as an answer to the last two questions above. If so, this would need to be used as a kind of test run in coaching Ruth in trying to tackle this relationship and create change within it. However, I think that the most likely answer for Ruth to give at this point will be 'mother'. Michael will then be able to move into some direct coaching of Ruth in her relationship with her mother and in how change might be brought about within it. The following stages need to be worked through over the next few sessions:

1 As full a clarification as possible as to Ruth's experience of this relationship: its development, the feelings it arouses in her and, especially, her feelings of anger, grief and loss. Michael has already done a lot of work on this, but it needs clarifying and summarizing before he can safely move on to:

2 Building some empathy between Ruth's own experiences and those of her mother. Here it is very important that the work on the genogram showing mother's own position in the relationship system and the roles and experiences she has carried and endured has been as full as possible. Out of that material will, I suspect, come plenty of new ways of viewing mother which will lead in time to:

3 Helping Ruth formulate some specific questions/areas of concern which she would like to explore with mother. These need to be grouped and considered in terms of mother's likely response to them and of the method of exploration to be used. For example, it is more likely that Ruth's mother may feel able to respond to a general invitation to tell Ruth more about some situation in Ruth's childhood or in her own childhood that Ruth has little knowledge of, than to give a direct answer to why she had not been able to talk with Ruth about the abuse she suffered, or indeed to prevent it from happening (to take an extreme and rather obvious example). Also, Ruth's mother is more likely to be able to respond if Ruth can couch her request in terms of general interest and care for her mother than in terms of criticism or attack. Further, it might be easier for Ruth to ask and mother to answer through an exchange of letters rather than a face-to-face conversation in the first instance, if this kind of opportunity were naturally to occur through a brief absence from home on Ruth's part. Because Ruth is still living at home, it might be particularly important to take a step back in the process and ask her mother whether she would be prepared, or even welcome the opportunity, to talk about some personal matters relating to the family. Doing this by letter might give her mother more time to give a considered response. Coaching Ruth in approaching her mother on these matters might take the form of some role play in the session, with the therapist acting the part of her mother and Ruth trying things out until they arrive at the approach which feels most likely to lead to a positive response on mother's part.

Inviting the family in for a session

The third and boldest possibility is to see if there is any mileage in getting a family session set up, in the first instance between Ruth and her parents and then maybe between Ruth, her parents and Stephen. This could naturally follow on after the work on the first two approaches to family work had been accomplished as outlined above. The fundamental thinking in all three of these approaches to Ruth's family is the same: Ruth will not be able fully to separate from her birth family (either physically or emotionally) until she has fully joined it – that is, until she has gained a 'good enough' experience of emotional closeness that has been hitherto impossible. Thus the overall aim behind a family therapy session would be to:

1 Build some mutual understanding of the different experiences which family members have had within the relationship system.
2 Pinpoint some issues that everyone could agree on as needing some more work and exploration.
3 Enable Ruth to leave home and establish herself within her own partnership, home and area of work with as good a relationship with her parents and brother as it is possible to achieve.

Further reading

Allen, D.M. (1994). *A Family Systems Approach to Individual Psychotherapy*. London: Jason Aronson.
Andersen, T. (1987). The reflecting team: Dialogue and meta-dialogue in clinical work. *Family Process*, Vol. 26, pp. 415–428.
Bentovim, A., Gorell Barnes, G. and Cooklin, A. (1987). *Family Therapy: Complementary Frameworks of Theory and Practice*. London: Academic Press.
Boszormenyi-Nagy, I. (1987). *Foundations of Contextual Family Therapy*. New York: Brunner/Mazel.
Carter, E. and McGoldrick, M. (1976). Family therapy with one person and the family therapist's own family. In P. Guerin (ed.), *Family Therapy*. New York: Gardner Press.
McGoldrick, M. (1989). Genograms and the family life cycle. In E. Carter and McGoldrick (eds), *The Changing Life Cycle*. Boston, MA: Allyn and Bacon.
Walrond-Skinner, S. (1979). Education or training for family therapy? A reconstruction. In S. Walrond-Skinner (ed.), *Family and Marital Psychotherapy*. London: Routledge and Kegan Paul.
Walrond-Skinner, S. (1988). *Family Matters*. London: SPCK.
Whiffen, R. and Byng-Hall, J. (1982). *Family Therapy Supervision*. London: Academic Press.
Young, J., Perlesz, R., Paterson, B., O'Hanlon, A., Newbold, R., Chaplin, R. and Bridge, S. (1989). The reflecting team process in training. *New Zealand Journal of Family Therapy*, Vol. 10, pp. 69–74.

9

MICHAEL JACOBS AND RUTH

REVIEW AND RESPONSE

This supervision exercise has some major differences from normal ongoing supervision, and these unusual dimensions need to be acknowledged before reviewing the value of each of the different approaches in this book.

It is unusual, although not unique, for a counsellor or therapist to go for supervision with a person of a different orientation. Having said that, in some training situations (the British Psychological Society's requirement for the Diploma in Counselling Psychology, for example), it is mandatory to experience supervision in two different orientations. I have myself supervised person-centred counsellors and once a bio-energetic therapist, and certainly in the former case have found little difficulty. Sometimes I think my supervisees have found it more difficult than me, especially when I have too readily assumed their knowledge of the position I take, although I have also had it said that I am not nearly as 'psychodynamic' as they imagined: one wonders what their perception of psychodynamic was? Nevertheless, there can be no-one who has experienced supervision on the same session with five different supervisors! It is not a practice I would recommend, except for these purposes, since my mind has buzzed with conflicting ideas throughout the latter part of this process. It is my experience on the one hand that has provided me with a firm enough base not to be thrown into the mire of confusion, and my willingness on the other to experiment with some of the alternative approaches that are normally not part of my repertoire, as well as the patient and interested willingness of my client who has been subjected to all this, that has made this particular experience of supervision possible.

It is also unusual to have supervision for a one-off session, and only to meet a supervisor once. This is why Alan Cartwright chooses to call his role in the project consultancy rather than supervision. I have on occasion supervised someone for a single session, over a particularly difficult situation, or when the regular supervisor was not available and it was important to discuss the matter. But usually supervision is an ongoing process, where week by week, or month by month, the progress of one or more clients can be followed through. Neither does most supervision follow on at this distance from the session, nor is its application to the ongoing therapy such a long time both from the supervision and the session under discussion. The process here has necessarily been long and drawn out. What makes it valid is that key issues in long-term therapy tend to remain the same: psychoanalytic thought describes this process as one of working through, going over the same material time and again, from slightly different perspectives, with new information, and in respect of different situations arising in the client's life. Certainly with Ruth, although in many respects she had moved on considerably in the eighteen months between the original session and the period of reviewing these supervision contributions, some issues have remained, and they were indeed resurrected in their importance when going back with her to that original session.

Further, this particular process, whereby material was exchanged through the medium of word-processor disks and at intervals of some months, was not representative at all of the dialogic situation in most supervision, although there is some supervision that takes place through the exchange of tapes. The ability to reflect on the therapy session is normally added to by the possibility that the supervisory relationship can reflect the therapeutic relationship in what is known as parallel process. Even if, as I have suggested elsewhere (Jacobs 1996), this concept has become exaggerated in its importance, the chance of discussing 'live' with a supervisor means that a supervisee can quickly correct a false impression on the part of the supervisor; the supervisor can ask short but necessary questions of information; and suggestions made can be mulled over by both parties as they look at how best to apply the ideas which have begun to emerge in their supervision discussion. None of this could happen in this instance, or at least none of this could happen in an immediate and easily identifiable way. I have little doubt, however, that the keen eye of the reader who is familiar with this reflective process will find more than I or my supervisors have identified.

Finally, it is again unusual (although not in the case of family therapy) for a client to become so directly involved in the supervision process. Of course it is the client who is at the centre of all supervision, and it is surprising that all this discussion takes place without the client knowing much about it. But a therapist is unlikely to say, 'My supervisor suggests that we look at . . .'; he or she is more likely to disguise it as, 'I have been thinking about this since we last met . . .'. Indeed, many therapists will not even inform their clients whether or not they discuss them in supervision, unless the client is being seen as part of a training placement. In this case, clients are normally informed and their permission is sought to use their material both in supervision and where applicable in written case studies necessary for the trainee's examination and assessment. What became clear in this project was that for Ruth to be so much a party to all that passed between myself and the supervisors was not only proper (since she is so much part of the book, and in any case would see the contributions eventually in print), but in most instances proved a most useful sharing with her of the process, of considerable benefit to looking at herself from different angles.

Only in one respect did it prove really unhelpful, and this would in normal circumstances not apply in therapy. When I was asked questions by my supervisors I naturally tried to be as honest with them as I could be. Sharing that complete honesty with my client would not normally be my way of feeding back a supervision session into the therapy, or not at least until such point as I was able to put what I felt into the right framework, the right words, at the right time. It would normally have been mine and the supervisor's knowledge alone. Even where supervision is more openly discussed (as in some family therapy), my guess is that since this is known to be the situation from the outset, it influences the way therapist and supervisor discuss the family in their presence. Ruth had to suffer all that I blurted out on paper, and I regret this; although she herself commented, 'I recognize this would be unsuitable for many clients, but though Michael's feelings were painful to me, I am able to acknowledge that by sharing them I was treated maturely, respectfully, and with truth and reality. The "perfect" therapist does not allow the client to learn how to handle the adversity of relationships'.

There are, then, these differences from the usual patterns of supervision with which the reader will be more familiar. They certainly add another set of dimensions to the supervisory process, but they do not in the end, I believe, detract from this fascinating examination of how the different supervisors understood the session, and related to me as the therapist and Ruth as the client.

Self-supervision

Supervision provides the opportunity to learn how to be a better therapist; but it also teaches the therapist how to monitor her or his way of working without always bringing it to supervision (it is impossible to talk about every client and every session). Such monitoring takes place after the session, when writing up notes, or thinking about the therapeutic relationship; and it takes place with experience in the session, so that the therapist begins to function as her or his own 'internal supervisor', to use Patrick Casement's (1985) concept so usefully explored in *On Learning from the Patient*. The internal supervisor is always subject to the distortions which our own subjectivity gives it, and the external supervisor clearly remains a check on self-delusion about one's ability as a therapist, as well as provides that third eye which inevitably sees what the person too close to the session cannot see.

For me the session in question became one of intense scrutiny, and I had my own thoughts on it before I sent it to the supervisors, as well as when I began to address their questions to me. I also had a sense of wanting to give it to them, so that although I worked on it in one way, as an editor, I did not work on it in the detailed way I hoped they would. What I would have liked, particularly in retrospect, is a question about my own understanding of the session. Only one of them asked directly for my own thoughts. Prue Conradi put the question, 'In reading the transcript, do you feel particularly troubled by any one of your own responses?' It would have felt more true to my experience of the session had others asked for my reactions. As Ruth pointed out on reading this, I too wanted to be heard, perhaps just as much as she wants to be heard, and that in the language of my own orientation (the psychodynamic) my counter-transference matched her transference. The supervisors failed to pick this up.

I was painfully aware, particularly in typing out the transcript of the session, that some of my responses were muddled in their expression, and that they were far too long. I was not concerned (as Conradi was) that Ruth had spoken at length too, but I wished I had been more concise myself. I wondered whether this was in fact my usual style of responding, although I thought that it was in this case rather exaggerated in its verbosity. I can be very attentive and quiet in sessions, I can say much less; I can be more empathic, ask brief questions, etc. The typeset transcript gives a somewhat false impression of the length of our respective contributions, because Ruth speaks more slowly and I tend to speak rather rapidly. Even so, I said too much. I knew that I was anxious about the end of the session, which is partly why I had taken this session to my supervisors. I also thought that I might have said more than usual in order to try and give something to Ruth in her very distressed state. Quite what I could give her I was not sure (and only later in reading the supervisor's chapters did I see how much I needed to give her more empathy), although I did feel that in my tone of voice I was gentle and warm towards Ruth. In commenting on this observation, Ruth notes that 'in my protective, re-assuring nature I want to affirm you that you do not usually react as you did in the session under scrutiny. Perhaps your lengthy, muddled responses were copying my confused, muddled and anaesthetized emotions and need to share deeply'.

The image of the assault course and the jump between trees had already struck me as deeply evocative, and I thought afterwards that there was something here about therapy too, although I was not clear what it was, and I think I missed a real opportunity at that point. Nor did I see during the session what became clearer on reading the transcript, that Ruth's reference to not being able to cry in church might also have been about not being able to cry more with me (although she had been crying, and I was therefore not tuned in sufficiently to its possible meaning that there was much more grief yet to be expressed).

These were some of my thoughts. My main concern was still how to handle the type of situation which had come up at the end of this session, and which I made clear in the final comments upon it. I felt shaken by the experience, unsure of myself, and whether I had been right or mistaken to accede to Ruth's request for a hug. It was this, and I suspect also – although I did not fully realize it at the time – the sometimes intense loving feelings which Ruth had for me and my inability to meet them for her, that needed to be shared with my supervisors, to see what they would say. In the event, most of them pronounced fairly clearly on the side of my not meeting Ruth's wish for comfort through its physical expression, with Conradi remaining more open to the possibility, but mainly asking for a different kind of response from me. Ruth wondered as we reflected upon the different sessions that followed through the supervision chapters what would have happened had there been one supervisor who advocated the positive value of touch (as some do). She suspected that this would in fact have made her feel insecure, and that in the end my acceding to her wish for a hug was 'my abuse upon Michael: he had no opportunity to agree and he disentangled himself immediately'.

But these issues are only a small part of my response to the otherwise generous and helpful comments I received from my supervisors. Much more came out of the supervision of the session than I had expected. That, of course, is the way it should be.

David Livingstone Smith

This was the first of the supervision comments to reach me, and was therefore naturally the first I turned to: it also seemed preferable for

Ruth to start with a contribution which was quite critical of me rather than one in which she was herself also the subject of a supervisor's comments.

When I read through his comments, my first feeling was of being attacked, and I note that Smith himself is concerned at how to communicate with me without traumatizing me. He provides little comfort to me, and the support he offers the client is to leave therapy: and there is I think no part of what I said or did which appears to merit any approval. Even at the point where, using his particular approach, he finds what appears to be a positively toned remark about me (the surgeon showing care), he implies that it should not be there according to his way of thinking, and soon dismisses it. I wondered why I could not be allowed at least one piece of affirmation from the client! My reactions on the first reading were both depression and anger, and I wondered how this might have been different had we been meeting regularly, face to face. He is certainly not an unkind man. And on my second reading, I of course noted that he is concerned about the impact of his remarks; and that he ascribes some of my own way of working to my own experience of personal therapy: I can presumably blame *my* therapist! There is obviously some truth in the suggestion that my own therapy influences the way I am. My therapist said little, although when he did he would speak at length and put more to me than I could usually absorb. In other respects, the way I interpret and link past and present, for example, must in some respects be influenced by him; and I know that I often sit like him. Such is the power of identification.

It took a second reading for me to begin to feel less defensive, and to examine what Smith had to say in its own right. I had after all asked for supervision, and I should not expect to hear what I wanted to hear. I could see how much I had broken the frame of therapy, although I had no wish to impose any of the rules which I assume Smith would require of me: I will continue to change times if Ruth really cannot make her session (due to a hospital appointment, for example), and I will continue not to charge her for missed sessions. I see no reason to raise my fee, other than annual inflation requires, although I can see (as I did also with Conradi's supervision) that this leaves me with feelings that I must be careful not to let intrude in other ways. These decisions are my responsibility, and I must not punish the client for them; but neither do I feel, even after Smith's supervision, that they overly distort the course of therapy. That *may* make it impossible for me to use what he writes elsewhere, although I do not find that to be the case.

I normally attempt to understand what my own part is in the

process, and I could see how much of this I had missed, as Smith's account identifies point after point where Ruth might have been unconsciously talking about me. The consciousness of the possibilities of abusing her through exposure had occurred to me, and has remained present throughout: I suspect in this session they may have taken a back seat because of my awareness of Ruth's obvious distress, which I attached to the operation rather than to the project. I still think in that respect my emphasis on the actual operation was right, although I can see how one-sided it was to link it to past events and not sufficiently to the present project.

I also take the point that 'all psychotherapists work in ignorance' and that Smith does not therefore set himself up as the one who knows. It is also reassuring to read that there is a misunderstanding about the communicative approach, that it thinks that *everything* that is said is about the therapist. The difficulty for me remains that in reading his account of the session he does give the impression that everything is about me, and nothing about the client's part in the relationship; and what is written about me is in a negative tone. I am left thinking that what is and what is not about the therapist in the client's unconscious communication is very arbitrary, and depends upon the supervisor's view. Furthermore, although taking to heart much of what he writes, I find myself questioning the basis of his statement that a story can carry both an unconscious as well as its more obvious conscious meaning. What if the two conflict? For example, Ruth said that she had turned down two other offers to help because they had felt pressurizing, but that I was not. If the unconscious is telling me that I am pressurizing, how does that square with her conscious message that by contrast I am not pressurizing. I cannot be both (unlike love and hate in ambivalent feelings, which can of course co-exist).

I miss any understanding of why I might be reacting to Ruth in the way I do – why it is that I miss most of what she was telling me. One explanation he gives is my own therapy being inadequate (which is certainly not how it feels to be, consciously); another more helpfully suggests that therapists make lengthy interventions when something is going on that frightens them. I was anxious in the session: anxious myself no doubt because of the tape-recorder (which now becomes clearer to me), but also more obviously anxious because Ruth was upset, and had come all this way to see me so soon after her operation because she wanted comfort, and I did not know how best to give it to her. I am sure that my lengthy interventions (which everyone identifies) and also my somewhat heady interventions (which Cartwright and Conradi in particular identify) owe something to my feeling as anxious as Ruth did, especially about her vulnerability. It was my anxiety at the end that led to my confusion as to how to respond to the wish for an embrace, and it is that which I took to supervision. I feel little supported in my anxiety, especially when I am told how badly I responded. Interestingly, I find myself in somewhat combative mood at times with Smith, which I think is not unusual in some supervisory relationships, and I felt at one point like saying that his one suggested intervention, 'You've just asked me whether I can do anything with what you have been saying . . .', is equally long. But my more rational response tells me that his words are a useful collating of many of the issues which Ruth had been expressing, delivered after, as he suggests, keeping silent for much longer than I was able to in this session.

In the end, what I find myself left with is a greater consciousness of and indeed appreciation of Smith's central message to me – that I should listen for the stories Ruth tells me, as unconscious communications about the here-and-now process between us. That is not foreign to my way of working, but I recognize just how central this is to the communicative approach, and that the unconscious communication might stretch much further than I am normally aware. My normal way is to listen to the client's expression of feelings about me, and to link these with other figures and experiences in the client's life, rather than fully recognizing just how much the client may be talking about me, and me alone. It seems to me one of the strengths of Langs' theoretical position (which Smith's supervision represents well) is to identify what are called 'non-transference' remarks by the client, and not to assume that they are purely 'transference'. I have, I think, been rather more attuned to this type of listening and intervention since.

When I gave Ruth Smith's chapter, I said that I thought this was going to be a strange and perhaps a painful experience for both of us, and that this supervisor was someone who was quite critical of me for not hearing what she was really saying. I was aware that Smith himself had cited Fairbairn and suggested that patients 'often consciously idealize their therapists while unconsciously criticizing them'. I therefore asked Ruth to read it with as open a mind as possible, not feeling she had to rally to my defence, but to consider whether he may in fact be rightly critical of me. In my own mind I was by now partly open to her confirming Smith's argument, even if partly thinking he had been overstrong in his criticism, and overinterpretative of my apparent errors. I tried in the actual session in which I handed Ruth the chapter to stay with the side that was open to the supervisor, and to be particularly aware of any stories that might support his views. About one-third of the way through this session Ruth referred to being let down by someone who was due to be involved with her on a counselling project. I suggested that in the light of what I had told her about the chapter she may be feeling that I too had let her down. She replied that while she thought I heard what she said, I did not always appear to understand it. (This is again where Langs becomes confusing: Is Ruth referring here to my latest remark and saying that in it I did not understand her, because she was actually trying to talk about another situation? Or is she confirming that my remark was indeed right, that I had let her down by not understanding her?)

About two-thirds of the way through the session, this same 'story' came up again, and this time she referred to another aspect of it, in which the person who had let her down had spoken to a third party, but not directly to Ruth herself. She was angry about this. I suggested that she might be angry that I too had spoken to these supervisors, including this one, behind her back, and that she did not know what I had said to them. She then asked whether the chapters revealed what I had said to them. I replied that they did, and this made the situation somewhat different – it was all out in the open.

When we met the following week, Ruth said she had found herself stirred up by Smith's chapter. In the first place it brought back the session which had pre-occupied me ever since, but which for her was largely history. It brought back the feelings she had had then: part of these included the re-appearance (not that they were ever absent for long at this stage) of her sexual feelings towards me. These all seemed to be issues which needed to be talked through, since they had clearly not disappeared from the agenda. She also felt that the question of therapy and faith (or, as in her dream in the original session, almost therapy *versus* faith) had been neglected by her, and she wanted to come back to this. She proceeded to tell a story about her vicar preaching on 'real fatherhood' and how when he was young he had a distant father from whom he wanted a hug – and she had wanted to give him one, because she identified with him. This in turn led on to her wishing that she could have a real father, one whom she could get close to. I suggested that I was really a therapist, and were I her real father she might well expect me to hug her, and not to do so would be rejecting. But since she wanted a hug from me, perhaps she was saying she wanted me to be her real father. She responded to this by saying that even with her father if she as much brushed alongside him it didn't feel right. With me she wouldn't mind that at all! What was perhaps also behind this story was her wish to protect her vicar who felt unloved. She may have felt that I too, as a result of this supervisor's chapter, felt unloved, and that she wanted to protect me. I saw this possibility after the session had finished; otherwise, I think I would have put it to her at the time.

The other major feature of her response to Smith, which in fact came to her first on reading it, was some anger with him for presuming to understand what her unconscious communications meant. She felt as if she was being told by him what she was really saying to me. Although she was aware of the danger of springing to my defence (I wonder as I write if she thought we could become allies against a third person intruding?), she said that in the session under review I *had* responded to what she was *actually* saying – that is to what she was consciously saying – and that I had responded well. She continued (I thought quite persuasively, even given my wish to be affirmed!) that it was vital to her that I did respond to what she was consciously saying, because she had never been responded to in that way by her parents. This seems to me a very important point, and a very telling criticism of psychoanalytic practice generally that it can pursue the unconscious meaning sometimes to the exclusion of conscious and reality issues.

Ruth could see that Smith's comment about me saying too much was accurate, although she thought that on that particular occasion she needed me to say more than usual; in fact, she went on to say that had I been the sort of therapist she has read about, who says very little, she would never have stayed at the beginning. The more I think about the session, the more I think she is right in this, and that I was struggling, in how much I said, to comfort her; and in so doing saying more than I would usually. As it was, on that original occasion, she felt my responses were accurate and comforting.

We were nonetheless able to look at her difficulty with me not responding: it was as if silence meant to her that I was not listening to her, and she needed to know that she was being heard. She also felt that Smith's observations about the process of being looked at by all these supervisors was a valid reading of her materials about the operation. This appeared to be of *interest* to her, but she was not apparently over-anxious about this aspect.

The suggestion that she should leave therapy with me, however, angered her. She implied that she could not go anywhere else, and that in fact she had spent two years before coming to see me struggling with these things on her own: seeking therapy was a huge step, in which she wanted to share this struggle with someone. She could not go back to being on her own again. (There was later in this process a quite different response in her when she read Conradi's contribution, in which I had revealed my own feelings about the indeterminate ending: she then got very angry with me.)

Ruth's responses, like my own initial reactions when I read the chapter, were about the obvious content of the session; it was harder for her to get hold of the idea, particularly in so consistent a form in Smith's chapter, of the unconscious communications in her material. It is to be expected, because what is in a person's unconscious is not easily going to become conscious to them: it would not need to be unconscious were it easily acceptable. Nevertheless, I had wondered whether David Smith's interpretations might hit a chord with Ruth, if not throughout, at least on occasion. I would expect after a supervision session to try out some of the ideas arising from the supervisor's remarks, and for some of them to be proved accurate. In this instance, Smith put himself on the line with clear assertions about what Ruth's hidden communications meant: he was of course referring to a session eighteen months previously, and it might be difficult for her to recall sufficiently to be able to own unconscious communications then. It was nevertheless disappointing to me (having thought myself that there was something in Smith's criticism of me for not hearing her) that there was little sense that Ruth saw him as an ally to her unconscious communication.

She agreed more with Smith's suggestion that in the original session I was being somewhat seductive; even then she thought that I was sometimes as worried by her sexual feelings for me – perhaps because she talked about wanting to act them out – as she was herself anxious about them. She thought in fact that I was not good at helping her express those feelings. Furthermore, as she talked about this aspect, Ruth refined her opinion, saying that were I indeed to make a seductive approach to her in what I said, she could see herself welcoming it. She had not in fact felt me to be seductive; the thought that I may have been excited her, but also made her wonder how she had come to miss what some of my supervisors had seen. Perhaps, she mused, she missed such signals from other people as well?

Trying to follow Smith's suggestion through, I pointed out to Ruth that what I consciously avoid, because of my concern (as it seems to me) not to abuse her, might in fact come through unconsciously. She responded that although it appeared as if I had introduced the sexual element into that original session, in fact there was plenty of evidence of her sexual feelings before the session and since. These were feelings that came from her: I was not therefore introducing my own agenda. She thought I was more comforting than sexual. She told a story at this point about two former boyfriends who were very gentle, although it was they who took the initiative in sexual matters. Once again this story appears (using this communicative approach) to be about me being gentle, but still taking the initiative in sexual matters – the unconscious counterpart to the conscious denial she had just made of my sexual seductiveness. But even this possible interpretation was frustrated in the next sentence when Ruth went on to say that in relation to therapy with me she herself felt that she had taken the initiative, and made me take her on. That was something she could do in some situations, and might be off-putting to people. Again, do I deny Ruth this insight into herself, on the grounds that she does not recognize what her unconscious is apparently telling her?

Just as a therapist cannot magically take down a client's defences simply by observing their possible existence, it may have been a forlorn hope on my part that it would work to suggest to Ruth that in reading Smith's chapter she should not become defensive of me. At least one of her stories in this session where she responded appears to suggest she wanted to protect me: later her anger with me became clearer, and she might have been reacting against this anger when she read of someone else's criticism; therefore she could not fully own the validity of Smith's argument. I have to allow this as a continuing possibility. Nevertheless, the problem which I experienced throughout the reading of this supervision of my work, and which Ruth also experienced, was that it is impossible only to listen for unconscious communication. It is equally impossible to ignore the obvious, and by implication impossible not to recognize that the conscious, too, is a true expression of thoughts and feelings in their own right.

The problem with following this way of thinking through is that as a therapist I begin to wonder whether anything is a true statement, and I start thinking that everything must be turned on its head. I therefore am led to doubt whether Ruth meant what she said in her response to David Smith. Since the communicative approach takes such a pessimistic view of the ability of most orthodox psychodynamic therapists to get anything right, surely it cannot be possible that Ruth's response is really telling me that I did get at least some of it right? When she tells me that she herself feels that the important thing is to be heard on the conscious, obvious, manifest level, and that to go beneath that is *not* to hear her, and is to reject her statements as much as her parents have always done, then I wonder (as in a sense the communicative approach is also saying) whether she as the client is the one who has got it right.

I am sure I have not got it all right. Ruth certainly saw some valid criticisms in Smith's assessment of my work, although his sense of pessimism about my work she found 'most frustrating and sad . . . insecure, unable to control, which in turn makes me angry with him and the unchallengeable, presumptive nature'. When she says this

I need to ask whether it is my unchallengeable presumptive nature she is in fact angry about, not his. I acknowledge, too, that of course he wrote to me and not to her, and it would for him, I imagine, be quite 'out of the frame' for the supervisory relationship to impinge upon the therapy relationship in such a direct way. For myself his chapter underlined the importance of listening for the constant stream of hidden communications about myself as a therapist: I have found since working on the chapter that I have become much more aware of this dimension, although constantly having to remind myself of it, because it is so easy to forget and to suppress ways of understanding material which casts me as the therapist in a less than favourable light. I continued to introduce such interpretations as together Ruth and I worked through the other supervision chapters.

I do not, however, agree that in the therapy I am abusing Ruth as totally as Smith states, nor that for this reason the best move Ruth could make would be to terminate therapy with me at once. But if it is possible to take such a supervisory stance and this theoretical position of Langs' with a little pinch of salt, in other words not to accept the communicative approach as being the sole way of understanding the client's material (and, to take Smith at his word, to accept that not '*everything* that patients say is *really* about their therapists'), this supervision has helped me to see ways in which I can abuse Ruth. This I can do partly through the whole process that is this book, something of which I have been aware throughout and have consciously worked hard to avoid, even though I recognize how the unconscious is not tamed by conscious will alone. I recognize also another kind of abuse, which is not hearing Ruth, or not hearing the additional meanings in her communications. As Ruth said to me with regard to a later supervisory contribution, 'neglect is also abuse'.

Alan Cartwright

This is consultancy, not supervision, where, as Cartwright says, the supervisor has responsibility for both the therapist and the patient. This in itself raises an important question, addressed by Richard Jones (1989) in his article in the *British Journal of Psychotherapy*, as to whether supervision is principally for the therapist or the patient. Jones comes down on the side of it being for the therapeutic relationship between the two.

When I heard the tape myself, and then transcribed it, I did not feel in Cartwright's words 'a tendency to perform for the tape', at least not in any sense of trying to be perfect; rather, I have since wondered, as I have written above, whether I was unconsciously anxious about the tape, and overdoing my attempts to be helpful. I take the point that the anaesthetic may have put a completely different gloss on the session, which I failed to recognize. On the other hand, I felt it was very important to be there for Ruth's usual session if she wanted to come. There was no pressure on her to do so. I accept that it may not have been a typical session, although I think that all the themes in it and the problem of the hug made it seem so. Probably what made it different for me was in acceding to the request for a hug, because I sensed the way she was feeling after the operation. At a more normal time I might have been more sure of my ground in saying no.

Cartwright discusses the narcissistic personality – the damaged self. Ruth sometimes appears to want her needs to be met without any thought for me, the therapist. She overrides her knowledge that I do not want a hug. This seems demanding when it happens, although it is worth contrasting this with her wish to give me love when she feels much better; for example, since that time, when she has been away working, she has wanted to share the good experience with me in a generous way. It has felt very different for her, she says, and indeed it feels different in therapy too – and interestingly it does not give rise to any desire to express the love physically. I see the difference between that state, when I am much more in Cartwright's description of Kohut's concepts, an 'independent object' and other times when I become a 'need satisfying object'.

Cartwright stresses that therapy is a corrective experience rather than a repeated experience. Change starts 'from the quality of the patient's selfobject experiences'. I have come to see the increasing importance of this side, although I think it is not as clear-cut as that. For example, I note that some of the 'good' things I give to Ruth cannot be accepted by her, and that this is a repeat of the experience she has herself had in the past when others have not accepted what she wanted to give them: this time, when it happens, it is her that does it to me. So, for example, in the work on Fennell's negative automatic thoughts, we find that despite the obviousness of my attention to Ruth outside the session through this whole project, she can still think to herself that I only think of her in the session. It is difficult for her to accept how much attention I give to her (as a therapist of course, not as a lover) outside the session. Cartwright himself suggests that I am repeating the past trauma in the transference by pushing her away. Perhaps this is so, although in the relationship between us I believe that my counter-transference may be partly one which is a response to her transference, which believes that I will push her away, and which leads to an expression of her desire that to some extent inevitably fulfils the prophecy. I do have a dilemma, and it is one which I expressed in presenting the session, of how on the one hand to respond without being intrusive, and yet without contributing to frustrated sexual wishes; and also on the other hand not being rejecting and denying her the comfort that she needs.

I agree with Cartwright that my interventions have (or can have) a didactic quality to them. Conradi sees them as intellectual, as 'head' rather than empathic, or about feelings. This is I think part of my own personality: that how things come about fascinates me, and my enthusiasm to understand can sometimes be over-expressed in that direction. The attempt to understand, I hope, conveys itself to the client as also being caring. I may however miss affirming the feelings. Having said that, in the first part of the session I try to get to what seems to me to be a conflict of feelings within Ruth, which Cartwright also acknowledges, saying that therapy is part of 'this conflictual framework'. I take his point about my not exploring those feelings sufficiently, and I can see the cues that are telling me what I am missing, for example that I am not a soul-mate. Perhaps my anxiety about her wish for me as a sexual mate has stopped me from seeing that. I refer above to my own spotting of Ruth's reference to her anxiety about what will be thought of her if she cries in church. Although she shed many tears in that session, and does so at other times, I failed to pick up her anxiety about this.

Cartwright goes on to say that she wants calming and safety, but expects coldness and exploitation. I agree that this is what Ruth expects, although I do not agree that she gets coldness and exploitation from me, which is I think one of the fears that several of the supervisors have. I do not think I am cold, and indeed Cartwright says elsewhere that my voice is 'cuddly' – he may mean by this that I am being sexually seductive, although my own understanding of it is that I am trying to be comforting in my tone of voice as well as in what I express. The danger is that my interventions, even if they are delivered with a tone of care and concern, are not enough. I can see that making links for Ruth is not enough. In fact Ruth also makes links, and has done so in her own self-analysis since before she met me. Although I have to consider the possibility that she does so because that is what she knows I expect her to do, and that such a way of thinking may be a way of pleasing me, I have also at times experienced as hard her and my attempts to reach a therapeutic relationship that meets her needs, and which recognizes my own as well. There can sometimes be a conflict of interests. Since my own wish is not to hug the client (or indeed any client), the insistence on it can feel (as Ruth herself is indeed quick to acknowledge) an abusive approach on her part too.

I have a concern, arising from both Cartwright's and also Conradi's comments, that I might abuse the client not just by asking her to take part in this project, but also by the way I apparently introduced sexual material into the session at its beginning. Cartwright says that the introduction of this material is not supported by the text, and he asks whether there ever was any evidence for an erotic trans-ference. Conradi appears to say something similar when she writes that I introduce 'rather loaded words or ideas that Ruth had not even used herself, like "dangerous" . . .'. The difficulty here is that it *is* in the previous text, or the sub-text of earlier sessions, and indeed it comes later into this one (assuming, as it is not possible to do with confidence, that the later reference is independent of any mention of it on my part). According to Smith's interpretation, the material about the operating theatre is a response to my interven-tion about sexuality, which has to be considered as a possibility. Nevertheless, as I say in the introduction to this session, I think it is abundantly clear that it was Ruth who introduced the sexual theme into the therapy, very early on, perhaps even before the first session, in her early fantasies about me before we first met. I also made it clear in the introduction to the session that the operation had been anticipated in sexual terms by Ruth in an earlier session, when we first started taping. While this may have been an uncon-scious communication about taping, as Smith suggests, it was also a clear link to her earlier abuse, one which I took up in the session following the operation. Given that there is continuity from session to session, I believe that a therapist can make interpretations in one session, even early in it, based upon previously revealed material. The sexual reference is not necessarily therefore in this case intro-duced by me. This seems to be overlooked by these two supervisors.

I like Cartwright's restatement of my confused message [5 M.J.], particularly the phrases, 'the dangerous man' and 'the therapist man'. But he also says that I cannot tolerate being experienced by Ruth as cold and that I therefore have to convince her that I am warm. That again is not the way I experience it: my tone of voice is a tone of voice I use in other sessions too. Indeed, some people have told me that my speaking tone is like they imagine from the title and con-tent of my first book: a 'still small voice'. I speak gently on most occasions. In the end I find myself muddled in reading Cartwright as to whether I am cuddly, warm, sexual or cold.

'At no point', he writes, 'does the therapist acknowledge comfort is not sexual'. I think I do, as quoted in [18 M.J.]: 'Why shouldn't you have it [comfort]?' I can see nevertheless how sexuality (which is there in the original abuse, and is there in Ruth's fear of intimacy, and is there in some of her feelings for me) is confused by me perhaps more than her, with calm, secure and comforting experiences.

Cartwright observes that the acting-out at the end of the session is a reflection of Ruth's discontent with the quality of the selfobject transference. That too I acknowledge and find helpful; I feel after reading his comments that I am not in fact 'holding' Ruth well enough, despite my saying to her that I do. Conradi seems to make a similar point. It is worth noting, however, that Ruth does not consider this to be a sufficient explanation for her wish for physical contact.

In his conclusion, Cartwright makes an assumption about my working methods. I think he has partially misunderstood me. My own therapy was in the middle tradition of British psychoanalysis, although my principal supervisor was of the Freudian (and Anna Freudian) school. This learning remains with me, as indeed Smith suggests it might. In fact judged by a pure Freudian approach, I completely neglect the father transference in this session, and it would be one of my own criticisms that I do not make enough of this in my work with Ruth. My training supervisor would have said that to me, I am sure! It is the mother relationship that gets my attention, although I agree that I am traditional inasmuch as I make interpretations linked to the repetition of the past. I see Ruth's anger as being more at the frustration of her comfort needs, not of her erotic needs; however, I do add from time to time (not in this session) that I think she can also sometimes be angry at my not meeting her needs sexually as well. Nevertheless, Cartwright's final words are a perfect summary of my intentions following working on his contribution: I need to speak less, attend more, and allow Ruth's statements to modify my assumptions. That I find an extraordinarily useful injunction.

Ruth's initial reading of this chapter was that she 'wanted to be free to be me' and felt that this supervisor really wanted her to be free too, by my tuning in to her. So she wanted to be heard. When she came to her session after reading Cartwright's chapter, she described how she wanted to be free enough to give me a hug, and for it to be accepted by me for what it was; and that it was not an attempt at breaking the boundaries. She disputed that it could be called acting out, because her intention was that she should be giving and loving towards me rather then getting something for herself. But before she came in she had a 'phone call to her at home, which had felt like the caller was harassing her. She then realized that her wish to come and 'be free' could also be taken by me as harassment. So freedom and truth, she concluded, cannot be heard: 'whatever I do has got be acting out'.

Yet the hug, she said, is something real and physical in its intent. It is not to be explained away as this supervisor does by saying that 'you are not giving me enough. It would be more fulfilling if it didn't become all encompassing as it has done in the past'. As to the comment that I am not tuning in to her, Ruth said that she felt I *was* empathic: 'I want to say, hold on, there are needs, and I feel you understand that. You are not giving me what I want, but it isn't that you are not tuned in!'

Ruth made her own interpretation of Cartwright's chapter, which was not the same as mine. What the difference perhaps illustrated was that the conflict between us about me not giving her physical warmth had not gone away. Each of us felt that Cartwright's consultancy had supported our own view of the matter.

Melanie Fennell

My own impression in first reading this chapter was how much work this was going to mean for me as well as for Ruth. It meant extracting information from all I knew about her, as well as structuring the information, although in this particular instance Melanie Fennell had already given some very full examples, which to some extent saved me doing the work, at least in the first instance. In fact after my first session using Fennell's ideas, I had the 'homework task' of re-typing Fennell's conceptualization of Ruth (see Fig. 1), so that I could give this to Ruth in its amended form, to see if it would be a more accurate and precise statement of her position. Interestingly, one of Ruth's negative automatic thoughts which emerged in the course of working on Fennell's suggestions, was that I did not think about her outside the session. She saw the evidence that I did in the typing up of the revised conceptualization (see Fig. 5), as well as in typing out the diary of emotions and thoughts. But without this evidence she might have remained convinced that I forgot her. This work, outside the session, took considerable time both for Ruth and myself; and those who are in private practice, or who contrast the relative costs of different therapies, need to allow half as much time spent in analysing and typing out the conceptualization (for example) as they have spent in the actual session with the client. I suspect the amount of 'homework' the therapist needs to do, especially after early sessions, is considerable.

In the course of this I came to recognize not just how active cognitive behavioural therapy could be in the session, but just how much precise thinking it asks of the therapist as well as the client, something which my own approach does not normally require except

Early experience
Little support/encouragement from parents/brother – distant, critical
Sexual interference from brother. Rape age 8 by brother's friends
No help from mother – 'grow up, don't be
silly' – felt ignored, uncared for
Abuse mixed with closeness/physical contact I needed – confusion
(although now I can *choose*)
↓
Absolute assumptions (schemas)
Men are dangerous/abusive/take advantage of vulnerability (40%)
I am vulnerable (?not good enough?)
(not important?) (doesn't apply)
No-one can be trusted (90%)
No-one cares about me, or will look after or protect me
(this can be 100% unless I am affirmed, when it drops – I can
recognize this one more now)
I want to add: Nobody will hug me; nobody will love me
No-one can really hurt me (100%)
↓
Conditional assumptions
If I let people get close, they will hurt or abuse me
(if M.J. did, he wouldn't abuse me. I can't be pushed right under)
I must always keep people at a distance (this is not true)
If I am not in control, I am not safe
(I suspect this is true although I would prefer to say 'a little bit
unsettled'; I am not worried about safety in regard to sex)
The only way to get closeness or comfort is to expose myself to
abuse (this is not true)
I want to add: If I speak up for a cause,
I will be made to look a fool
↓
Critical incidents
Originally: Road accident, orderly's reaction,
parents' slowness to visit
Now: Treated as second best by mother, circumstances of
redundancy, illness/no visitors or signs of care, operation and its
aftermath, not being given affection/comfort by Michael
↓
Negative automatic thoughts
I want to be cared for and comforted (true)
Who can I trust? (not true)
Not even Michael will give me what I want (true)
Where will it all end? (true)
Will I ever be able to trust anyone? (I can trust)

←→ ↑ ←→

↓

Emotions	*Body sensations*
Vulnerable, exposed, sad	Cold (doesn't apply now)
(the first two words are less true,	Tense, uptight
although in the session reported	Tearful (this is not negative;
I *was* vulnerable)	there was a time I could not cry)
Angry, frustrated	Frightened, alienated

Behaviour
Withdraw from people, hide feelings,
avoid close relationships, cry
(these aspects are now changing; I am improving in
getting closer)
I want to add: I tend to analyse things too much

Strengths/assets/qualities
Courage, persistence, hard worker, articulate, self-aware, ability to
make a career, ability to make positive relationships (Frank, Brian,
Michael)
I want to add: I can be caring and loving, quite warm and giving

Implications for therapy (possible points of difficulty)
Wanting to be held, loved, make love, give love,
temptation to break boundaries
(I agree that this is certainly the biggest difficulty)
Anger/frustration when needs not met
Difficulty trusting/tolerating closeness (this is not really true)
Likely to see therapist as untrustworthy, cold, critical
(No, I find Michael trustworthy, and cold only in relation to being
held and loved. Is he critical? I would say rather he is challenging
things that I feel unable to change, and I can feel at a loss,
because I don't know what to do next)
I want to add: There can be tenseness in the relationship: Michael
worrying whether I am going to push him to break the boundary

Figure 5 'Ruth's conceptualization', as amended by Ruth

in preparation for supervision, or perhaps in a periodic review of
the case notes. It was not simply that I was being asked to change
my approach; in fact, I felt some relief that Melanie Fennell was
suggesting something positive, in much the same way as it turned
out Ruth did. (I did not have to be convinced through the exercise
that Fennell set me towards the end of her chapter – I was prepared
to try her suggestions without any pre-conceived ideas.) But the
degree of precise thinking about the material was new to me. Much
of my thinking about Ruth normally (outside the session as well as
within it) might sometimes have been both dogged and vexed, but

none the less it tended to weave round rather less precise hypotheses, and in any case awaited confirmation from Ruth, which might then allow me to put my thoughts across, rather than as in this case putting my ideas to her first, for her to consider them.

Ruth felt, and it was certainly the experience of using Fennell's chapter, that she gave us something to work on and that it encouraged cooperation. Out of the three so far this was the one that Ruth herself could most enter into, but of course this was part of the therapeutic approach that came through in supervision, whereas the first two supervisors were speaking to the therapist, and not to the client directly.

Ruth perceived this as a positive approach, and one that had made her realize that she hadn't recognized what an open-ended way we had been working in. The result of reading it was that she rose to it: it was helpful, contained specific ideas, although she was not sure she would have been able to recognize her negative behaviour and automatic thoughts without someone to help her (of course, this is what the therapist does). But there was a sense now of knowing this, like the way I had also observed to her that there were repeated patterns. Yet being able to change out of them is quite hard. Ruth could see them, but getting round them was another matter.

Thinking about her core beliefs, on a scale of 0–100 per cent, Ruth noticed that where she was 100 per cent negative was in statements like: 'I can never be loved'; 'I can't express myself'; 'I can't ever get tactile affection/affirmation'; 'I'm not worth it'. But this can soon get dispersed from being 100 per cent if she is encouraged in what she is doing. And if someone affirms her, that more extreme desire for the therapist fades. I wondered myself whether this confirmed Cartwright's recommendation, that more affirmation by the therapist would mean that she did not need to act out the need for physical contact.

Ruth said that she saw that she could cope without physical contact, but so far what she had received from reading the supervision chapters was that everyone was telling her (through me) that she should never expect closeness. This was not the perception I had of these chapters, but it clearly had lodged itself as a further negative assumption in her mind.

This was a very active session – the time positively flew, and we were soon reaching the end of the hour, with only a part of Fennell's recommendations discussed. Ruth felt positive, although she wondered whether she wanted sessions which were regularly like that; and wondered whether it would be so good all the time. It helped to summarize where she had been on the occasion of that session, and the question of physical affirmation was still an issue, which she did not know how to deal with. She said there was a feeling of

Date	Emotion(s) What do you feel? How bad was it (0–100%)?	Situation What were you doing or thinking about?	Automatic thoughts What exactly were your thoughts? How far did you believe each of them (0–100%)?	Rational response What are your rational answers to the automatic thoughts? How far do you believe each of them (0–100%)?	Outcome 1. How far do you now believe the thoughts (0–100%)? 2. How do you feel (0–100%)? 3. What can you do now?
16 February	Put down, hopeless, inadequate (75%)	At college: fellow student looking at my work and making suggestions (she was reasonable/helpful)	'I might as well give up. I can't do it' (90%) 'I have to justify myself' (75%)	She is only trying to help (70%) I must find a solution, find the truth (80%)	1. 30% 2. Drained: 50% 3. Re-look at my work, challenge the tutor who is not giving enough help

(As we discussed this entry in therapy, we saw in the last point how Ruth introjected her angry criticism of tutor, and turned it on self)

Date	Emotion(s)	Situation	Automatic thoughts	Rational response	Outcome
16 February	(a) Resentful, helpless, some anger, irritated (90%) (b) Feeling dismissed, but then heard (1 think) (90%)	Challenging the tutor for more guidelines	(a) 'I want help – give it me now (80%), or I'll give up' (80%) (b) 'I'm not being listened to; don't muck me about' (90%)	It's the tutor who is disorganized – not me (90%) I don't know what I'm doing, but I can press him (80%) Others are in a similar boat (95%)	1. 20% 2. Less stressful: 40% 3. Patience – see if tutor does anything. If not re-do my work and keep pushing the tutor

(The result of this diary entry was that Ruth felt very positive; the emotions and thoughts did not stay with her; they were finished with and put aside, staying in the diary)

Date	Emotion(s)	Situation	Automatic thoughts	Rational response	Outcome
19 February	Inadequate, out of my depth; fear of making myself look foolish (80%)	Having to present information to a meeting with lot of more experienced counsellors than me	'If I go wrong this will affect my future' (90%) 'Why didn't I realize it was going to be a group like this?' (70%) 'I shouldn't be here. I am not big enough' (70%)	I'm here to learn. It is OK to make mistakes (70%) No-one here knew what this would be like – we are all in the same boat (80%)	1. 20% 2. 10% of what I felt before 3. I can do this. I will change my presentation to make it easier *(The result was that Ruth did it)*

Figure 6 Daily record of negative automatic thoughts

bitterness: 'I am a woman. Why can't I be held? I am annoyed that therapists say that touch isn't important'. She wanted to have a further session on her negative thoughts, which we looked at the following week. I also gave her some diary pages, set out as in Fig. 3, to complete if she thought this would be helpful.

A second (and a third) session was spent on the diary of emotions and automatic thoughts. One of these pages is reproduced in Fig. 6, which indicates how much Ruth was able to change her way of reacting and thinking through the suggested way of completing the diary entries. A second page (not reproduced here) contained a series of entries around one incident which was not so helpful: Ruth thought this might have been because the emotions were high, and she was still too close to them when she wrote the entry. This meant that she tended to keep slipping into negative automatic thoughts, even when trying to be rational and in rating the outcome. The incident involved a further feeling of being left without adequate help, which led me to suggest, towards the end of that session, that in addition to these incidents being recorded in the diary, she might also be feeling that I too had not given her enough help, even if this present method was proving more structured and therefore more helpful. I felt that I should not lose sight of the type of interpretation of unconscious material that David Livingstone Smith had urged me to be attuned to. Ruth (knowing my usual interpretations) could see this coming as I started to say it. Her reply was that she felt during this exercise that there was considerable collaboration between us, and that we were doing things together, which provided a sense of closeness. She got a 'buzz' from that. She also described how she had not experienced, during the process of working in this way, the thoughts of and pangs for closeness and intimacy that she did at other times. Does this bear out Cartwright's suggestion, that her wish for this is related to my lack of response? And that this method of working was not only active, but also positively responsive to her?

I also noted that there was nothing in the actual diary entries that she had produced which involved emotions evoked in her family, or in therapy. Ruth replied that there had been one incident, involving her mother and some financial help she was initially promised, but which was then withdrawn, but she had avoided recording it. The next week she retrospectively recorded it, and again the distance from the incident helped her to find more rational responses and a more positive outcome.

The following week was interesting. Ruth, of her own accord, had decided that she would follow through a very positive feeling, using the same system, and see what emerged. She had had a very affirming and exciting experience the day after our session, one which she wanted desperately to tell me about, her parents about and her friends about. As she recorded the incident and the emotions and went through the process of the rational responses, she found that this took the edge off her excitement. It was as if this approach had a way of dulling emotions – fair enough when they were negative, but in the end leading to a rather bland existence if you applied it to everything. Her experiment might be interpreted as having to spoil even the good things that happened to her, although I found it a convincing example of her enquiring mind, and an interesting perception of the method. Rational thinking is elevated above emotion, which may in the end lessen the normal ups and downs of living.

A further entry showed up another qualification which we both felt towards the method. Ruth was feeling very depressed at the approach of her fortieth birthday. This involved a number of aspects, including whether anyone would celebrate it (which we were able to look at rationally, and to plan some actions which would initiate this), but which also involved a huge sense of loss for what she had not been able to have – especially children. She had tried to rationalize that situation too, looking at her automatic thoughts, and finding a rational response which was: 'It's useless to feel that way'. The outcome included a further thought: 'I need to curb my selfish desires'. This in fact was yet another negative automatic thought, and it showed us how often she slipped into these, even when she was trying to be rational and positive. But the point remains that whether it was useless or not to feel the sense of loss, the sense of loss was there, and that it was important to remain in touch with emotions of sadness. What we could challenge was her self-criticism and her idea of her own selfishness.

We left the intense concentration upon this method the following week as we moved on to consider the person-centred supervision of the session. I suggested that Ruth continue to use the diary as she wished, and that if she ever wished to bring it to a session to discuss it, she should do so. I felt that it had highlighted patterns of thinking that would be easier to identify in the future, and in the course of working in this way I considered how valuable some training in cognitive-analytic therapy would be (see Ryle's contribution in the companion volume *Charlie*).

Prue Conradi

When I was presented at the second stage of this project with the questions which Conradi asked of me, I found myself in a dilemma.

I wanted to answer them honestly, because it is vital that a supervisee is completely honest in supervision. Only in that way can the fullest motivations and thoughts be expressed and worked with, even if unconscious thoughts and wishes clearly cannot be expressed solely by the intention to be honest. At the same time as I was answering her questions, I was dimly aware (although much more strongly later) that Ruth might read some of this, although, of course, I did not know at that time how much Conradi would choose to reveal in her chapter. I do not think I was quite aware of just how much of my answers she would reproduce. Had I known I might have been less generous with the truth, although, of course, as far as this project is concerned, that would be less helpful to the reader.

Despite some incipient reservations, I did answer as openly as I could, and when I had done so, I felt much easier in myself: it was a relief to share with Prue Conradi the frustration and the anger that had been building up in me, especially over the complaint from Ruth that in not giving her a hug I was not giving her enough. My anger was mine, and I do not claim that it came from Ruth or from her issues. But it needed to be voiced, and worked within myself, and even in voicing it (i.e. in writing it to Conradi) I felt more relaxed in myself, and much more generous in my feelings towards Ruth. Ruth later complained when she read Conradi's chapter that I should have done something about this 'festering anger', and she asked me whether I had taken it to supervision. Of course I had, I had taken it to Prue Conradi, whose questions to me enabled me to get in touch with how strong a feature it was within me; but I had not realized it was there to that degree until I began to answer this supervisor's questions. Before then it had been in me, but hidden in me, although spotted sometimes by Ruth (when she said she thought she made me angry) and only partially admitted by me either to myself or to her.

As soon as I received Conradi's contribution I knew I was going to have to 'face the music' with Ruth. I could not tamper with the chapter, asking the supervisor, for example, to cut out the questions and answers which would reveal so much to Ruth: that would have been unfair to Conradi, and would not indeed have revealed the value of the process. Neither could I hide my answers from Ruth, who one day would have to read them. I could only make it a little easier for myself by acknowledging that Conradi was right about the need for me to be more congruent, and more real. This was a test of whether I could take on board this particular emphasis in person-centred therapy; working together with Ruth on Conradi's chapter was a way of being able to do that. Ruth would learn how I *had* felt – and I think it was that, rather than the way I *still* felt, since the very act of writing it down to Prue Conradi had helped to identify and temper my strong feelings.

I handed the chapter to Ruth and I warned her that there were some remarks by me which I had made over a year previously, in the course of answering this supervisor's questions; that I had found it helpful to be able to express my feelings then to the supervisor; and that I thought that I had then been able to resolve them. I also reminded her, as I had with Smith's chapter, that any comments by me about her paying less (another of my resentments) was my choice, and my responsibility. I carefully ensured that we were meeting the following week (this was at a period when Ruth was sometimes going away to find work), so that I could give Ruth the chance to explore her feelings about the chapter more immediately. I thought that I might have hurt her by my own remarks, although I hoped that she would feel supported by Prue Conradi's comments on her.

As I predicted, Ruth was both hurt and angry when she read the chapter, although she had also taken Melanie Fennell's work to heart, and so she re-read the chapter, approaching it with a more 'rational' frame of mind. Ruth's ability to work on the material in this way was consistently remarkable, and she showed herself to be adaptable (perhaps even more adaptable than I) to different ways of approaching her therapy. Using therefore the supervision chapter we had recently been working upon, she was enabled to monitor her feelings and her ideas about this new chapter. She wrote them down for me lest she forget, although also I suspect to drive them home to me as much as my own written words had made their own impact on her.

She was very angry with me (as I have already indicated) for not telling her at the time I wrote to Conradi what I had felt about her then. I myself felt (and responded to Ruth thus, although perhaps rather hastily and therefore over-defensively) that supervision had been for me to work on my own agenda, and that since this had in this case been successful, normally I would never have needed to share any of my negative feelings with Ruth. Prue Conradi of course suggested that I be more real and open – more congruent – and it is possible that had the process been within the usual time-span, rather than drawn out in the way it inevitably was for this project, I might have said something to Ruth in order to remain congruent. But Conradi made a suggestion, and not a demand, and I am sure she would intend the timing of any sharing of congruence to be left to my judgement of the right opportunity.

Doing it the way we had done for the book had meant much of the subtlety one would expect of a therapist was lacking. Winnicott, for example, records how he was able to tell one of his patients the effect that he had had on him, but only when the man had come through this particular time of difficulty:

> It was indeed a wonderful day for me (much later on) when I could actually tell the patient that I and his friends had felt repelled by him, but that he had been too ill for us to let him know. This was also an important day for him, a tremendous advance in his adjustment to reality.
>
> (Winnicott 1975: 196)

I too have felt the value of telling clients, at such a time when they are strong enough to hear it, how they can be on other occasions or how they were at an earlier stage in the therapy, such as them then being more difficult to relate to. Ruth believed that these issues were still around for me, and she felt that handing her a chapter was a 'cop out'. She wanted me to say these things to her directly. For reasons just stated, there had in my view been no necessity for saying these things at the time, although I had since the correspondence with Conradi on occasion been able to share with Ruth my experience of her being more giving and loving in a non-possessive way, and how this was quite different from other times when she could be more demanding. There was, however, one area of being more real which I find it difficult to envisage I would ever have revealed to Ruth had it not been for this particular project. Ruth suggested to me that I should have told her about my concern about her paying less than usual rates. As I observed to her, I suspect that had I done so I would simply have used that feeling as a weapon, a tit for tat revengeful remark, at such times when she complained about me not giving her enough: what good would it have done to make her feel bad by saying something like 'I give you a longer session, for a lesser fee than I do normally'? I want to temper the value of being congruent with considerable caution.

Ruth also felt that I was treating her as an object, not as a person. Part of this feeling came though reading about herself in my eyes and seeing herself more as someone I 'worked with' (as I had written) than someone I had feelings for. Such a dichotomy is I believe a false one, because the work of a therapist necessarily involves feelings for a person, including the negative feelings which Conradi had helped draw out. These are of course more difficult for a client to take, even if in most relationships outside therapy, including intimate relationships, negative feelings are as much a feature as positive ones. What was difficult, and I suspect will remain difficult for Ruth, is that I see her because it is my work, and I do not see her because she is a friend, or because she is a potential lover. We initially met through her being someone I worked with, and therapy has continued this, even if she perhaps at one time entertained the fantasy that it might be more than that. This reality, that therapy relationships are primarily work relationships, lies behind all responsible therapy, even though the therapy relationship is highly unusual in the way it permits other ways of relating to be voiced. This also inevitably makes it a rather special relationship, although not as special as the intimate relationship which Ruth (and many other clients) are seeking. I return to this below. In Ruth's case, this strange relationship is made even stranger in that we have been brought even closer through working on this project, while at the same time the project is of course (as Smith observes) part of my work.

Ruth's reading of what I wrote to Conradi was that 'you treat my love with a pinch of salt' – that I rebuffed it, and made light of it. Drawing upon Fennell's suggestion of looking at these thoughts more rationally, I asked Ruth whether this really was so. Could she show me how I had done this? Was not returning her love in the way she wished, which I accepted was the case, the same as making light of her, and treating her with a pinch of salt? In the course of what was (in a very different way from the Fennell work) a fast and somewhat furious (perhaps somewhat literally furious?) session, we did not fully explore this, although this was a further opportunity to underline just how quickly Ruth turned her experience of me into negative thinking.

Ruth also angrily suggested that if I wanted to end the contract I should do so. She gave me her permission to do this. In fact, I reminded Ruth, my remark to Conradi about when it was ever going to end was just what she had also said to me: she too had sometimes said that she felt that it was getting nowhere. That was not the same as saying that I wanted it to end; indeed, I was in my own mind certain that I wanted to continue at least until the book was published, if that was her wish. This remark somewhat backfired on me, since Ruth took this as implying that my primary concern was for the book, and not (as I had intended) for her. Once again she felt like the object, not being treated like a real person.

I reflected to Ruth during this session that she had for a long time been saying that she could not get angry with me. There was no doubting her anger now, stirred up of course by my own, which she had read about in a way which (as I have already discussed above) might not normally have been made known to her in such a bald way. Nevertheless, there was a sense in this session in which Conradi's suggestion that I should be more real was showing its value.

There was one other area which Ruth felt angry about. She had read Prue Conradi's chapter carefully, and she had not understood her to be saying that I *should* touch Ruth. But she had picked up Conradi's ambivalence on the subject, and this in turn led her to pick up elsewhere on Conradi's concern that I might be abusing her. I had indeed abused her, Ruth told me, because I had abused her by neglecting her, and by withdrawing from her. Touching her would make her feel more a person than an object. She reminded me that touch was only part of what she felt – her love for me was 'intense, affectionate, tender desire, to be and to share with in an intimate way, not just physical. Sex is just the cream of togetherness'. What I became aware of when she said this was that even in the non-physical aspects of the love she was describing, I could not be all that she desired of me. In a real sense (to continue to use this somewhat unclear term) my response to Ruth, inevitably since I am her therapist and not her friend or lover, means that her love is unrequited. In this session I felt able to be true to myself and affirm that I was no longer concerned about the touch issue, because I was now firmly convinced that this was something I did not wish to permit in therapy; and at the same time I began to sense the reality of my being just a therapist (an object in my own right, if you wish) and not the person whom Ruth desired (and had always desired) that I be to her. That was an important part of my need to be able to be true to myself, and not to feel guilty that I had my own wishes about how I wanted to be.

At the same time I was reminded of a brief but telling passage in Ferenczi's notebooks. Ferenczi incurred Freud's criticism because he developed a technique which included holding and cuddling his patients and sometimes even kissing them. Ferenczi's reasons are no doubt more complex than suggested in this passage, but his words rang a bell:

It is my (the analyst's) fault that the transference has become so passionate – as a result of my coldness. A much too literal repetition of the father–daughter dependence: promises (fore-pleasure, gratifications, leading to expectations) and then nothing given.

(Ferenczi 1955: 262)

According to Ruth, by my coldness I make her more frustrated and more demanding. She admits my coldness is not total because she finds me a warm person. She does, however, see my stance over touch as rigid. Nevertheless, she also felt, as she said in the session in which we worked on Conradi's chapter, that the collaborative work we had done together previously on Fennell's contribution, as reported above, had led to a more open relationship between us, and one which had *lessened* her wish for physical contact. 'There was contentment in our closeness', Ruth said.

At this point, perhaps, some clarity is beginning to emerge, especially about the vexatious question of touch, and responding to Ruth's love. Working openly together, as Fennell's agenda had helped us to do, reduced the intensity of Ruth's need for physical closeness. We were together in a different way. Alan Cartwright and Prue Conradi do not set out any such collaborative programme of work, although they both urge a more empathic response on my part: they seem to suggest that responsiveness to Ruth's feelings through empathy (to which Conradi adds the value of congruence) will reduce the need to demand an acting out response. In a rather different way, Smith also urges me to pay real attention to what my client is expressing, although I am less convinced that his firm adherence to 'the frame' will help with Ruth.

I begin by this point to see what might have happened in the session which forms the basis of these supervisors' remarks. I tried to give, to respond to Ruth's wish for comfort, but I did it in the wrong way. For one thing, I spoke too much – it was one way of trying to give her something of myself; for another I tried to put things together, to 'sew things up' and make it better that way. Staying with her feelings, perhaps sharing more openly my own feelings in response to her pain, might have brought us together, and enabled Ruth to be heard, to be held metaphorically. Although that would not have been the same as reframing her thoughts and feelings in the way Fennell suggests, that could have been a further step, once the more immediate effects of the hospital experience began to ease. What Ruth clearly says is that one way or another she wants a response from me and a sense of being understood, something she did not have as a child when she most needed it. This in turn creates the possibility of a closeness which does not have to rely upon physical expression to feel real. It enables her to feel more fulfilled in the therapy relationship. When she does not have this sense of being understood and of being responded to, she experiences rejection and being treated like an object ('like a pinch of salt'); and not unnaturally she complains at the lack of response from me. When she does this I feel threatened by her criticism (especially when I see myself as *trying* to respond to her); and therefore I become less effective in my responsiveness, angry and perhaps even somewhat punitive.

While this holds together, I am aware that this intellectual construction does not remove the possibility that from time to time Ruth also returns, almost like a dog at a bone, and in a somewhat punitive way on her own part towards me, to the question of my physically holding her. That perhaps is her way of expressing the inevitable negative aspects there are to the therapy relationship, at any time when it reminds her of the lack of affection and understanding in her own family of origin. While sometimes this is in response to a genuine lack of understanding on my part as therapist, so that her feelings are real as well as transference, there are, I believe, also occasions when this happens as a result of Ruth's own interpretation of events, in the way she has been able to identify through Melanie Fennell's recommendations for examining negative thoughts.

It is interesting to me that Conradi's chapter, the effect of which on Ruth so concerned me, was in fact under discussion for just one week. It was, as I have noted, a 'fast and furious' hour, and I myself expected to return to it the following week. But we did not. It was as if the storm had blown over, and the issues which so vexed Ruth did not obviously appear again. Ruth later commented that this was partly because of her avoidance, since she thought that her anger had upset me, and that she had more to lose by expressing it: she wanted therapy to end on a positive note. But she also said, in contradiction, that the anger had been vented and laid to rest. For my part, I was glad both that she had an opportunity to express her anger, and that I had the chance to express my own responses clearly, although I too need to be careful not to avoid any of her angry feelings for the sake of a neat peaceful ending.

I believe that in the session in which we talked over Conradi's session we were both 'real', or in person-centred terms, 'congruent'. For the opportunity to express my own frustration and anger with Ruth (however undeserved on her part), and for the further opportunity for us to share our feelings with each other in response to Conradi's contribution, I am grateful. It was this which came out of her chapter more obviously than anything else. She got nearer than any of the other supervisors to working on my feelings in the situation, and through this helped moved the therapy on.

Sue Walrond-Skinner

Sue Walrond-Skinner's contribution to this project, as explained in the introductory chapter, came at a point when I had been let down by an original contact. As it turned out, choosing her was to provide me with yet another different perspective, one of which I had little experience or knowledge. Nevertheless, the idea that 'live supervision' in family therapy in some ways reflects the particular, and for me atypical, process described in this book (that is, sharing the supervision with the client) appealed to me as much as it did to this supervisor. What is evident is how much Ruth was able to use this supervisor's suggestions, as much as if the supervisor had come into an actual session. There may not be the immediate feedback from Ruth which Walrond-Skinner would have liked (just as there was no immediate feedback from me to the other supervisors), but there was no end of it in the sessions that followed Ruth's reading this chapter. I had in this instance given Ruth the chapter to read before a two-week break, knowing that the intervening time would be a good opportunity for the 'homework' suggested.

As a result of her agreeing to take part when the project was already well under way, Walrond-Skinner's chapter was, as expected, the last to arrive. It is difficult to know whether it was this fact, or whether it was the chapter in its own right, that meant that it acted as a summing up of the therapy to date. Following upon our work on Conradi's chapter, and perhaps pointing up the contrast in emotional tone, Ruth's initial comment on Walrond-Skinner's was that, 'It didn't provoke anything', although the evidence to me was that it provoked much, even if it was a very different response to the anger which had come out of our working through of the previous contribution. In one sense, Walrond-Skinner's suggestions had taken Ruth back to the start of her therapy. The counselling course she had attended before she first came to me had already asked her to look at her family tree. She had (the reader is reminded) initially worked alone upon her history, until she reached a point when she wanted to come into therapy to find help in taking it further. Walrond-Skinner's suggestions for my working with Ruth produced a considerable amount of historical information and a considerably enlarged genogram to that produced within her chapter from the scant amount of information I had provided. Ruth's written comments and genograms drew together, but with some reflections and extensions, all that we had talked about over four years. I myself might have been able to produce much of this, had I been as attentive in the records I kept as family therapists are to the details of the family and the history of the different generations. Ruth handed me seven pages of notes which she had made in response to the chapter. Fennell's chapter clearly had got her in writing mood, but there was even more here than she gave me following her reading of Conradi's chapter. Perhaps this was not surprising, since Sue Walrond-Skinner, like Melanie Fennell, had suggested I set particular tasks, and Ruth had responded with what I was consistently seeing as her real enthusiasm for learning. What was different this time from the first occasion, before therapy, when she had drawn up her own family history, was that this time talking about it was accompanied by great feeling. Ruth was aware that before therapy all she had was factual knowledge, but with no emotional response to it.

The other fascinating information which she shared at the start of our first review session on Walrond-Skinner's contribution was that she had on this occasion for the first time driven down to Leicester for her therapy session with her mother. She could not accept directly, as I shall show, the suggestion that the family come to therapy together, but that on this occasion at least Ruth came as near as she could to it. She said that she would be happy for me to meet her mother 'in the street, shopping in Leicester'. She had also talked with her mother on the ninety-minute journey, following through another of Walrond-Skinner's suggestions, that she explore her mother's history with her. Yet she felt for a variety of reasons that she could not contemplate family therapy. One was that she would not be able to talk about her sexual feelings for me, since it was impossible to talk about sex within the family – all that side would have to 'kept under wraps' if she was in family therapy. (I wonder whether the transference or even the real relationship with the therapist is ever as close as this in family therapy, and therefore whether such sexual feelings would have been as intense as they were in this one-to-one setting?) Ruth also did not wish to share me with them. She wondered whether it was really that important to build up the relationship with them so that she could leave them. She was not sure that she wanted to belong to this family in order to be able to leave them. She was not sure (although the evidence was to the contrary in what she produced for me) that she wanted to understand anyone else. She also did not want to be robbed of her anger.

Against this view of the value of family therapy, Ruth also saw herself as being the family healer, the reconciler, the protector of the family, although she wanted to have individual therapy for herself, not for the sake of the family. Nevertheless, the role she has adopted suggests she does want a family around her in which she experiences cohesion and belonging. She gave as an example of the reconciling function the way she was the only one who had kept contact with a family member, with whom her parents, her brother and herself had lived until Ruth was eleven years old. In her expanded genogram, which she produced for both sides of her parents' family, she also noted that she was the one who had initiated contact with other relatives on her mother's side. In her notes she said, 'I think I have played my part in drawing the wider family together, but this still presents a difficulty'.

While Ruth denied that the chapter had 'provoked anything', the sessions in which she talked a vast amount about her family were full of tears. She felt that she was crying over the loss of a family (as indeed Walrond-Skinner predicted the grief might be about), and the isolation that this had meant for her as a child and as an adult. She also saw that her mother had probably felt very isolated when she had married and moved away from a close family in her city of origin. Her father too had been fostered, but was not allowed to be adopted. Ruth was very aware that in trying to talk with her mother she did not want to create too much pain for her. It was clear that Ruth needed to protect her mother, including protecting her from all that Ruth had been through. There were new parallels that she could identify, and a new understanding of her mother, much as Walrond-Skinner had hoped might emerge. The experience of her family of origin (on both sides) was indeed as Walrond-Skinner had thought, that geographical distance from their own families of origin had led to emotional distance in their own immediate family.

Walrond-Skinner makes three suggestions as to how I should proceed. The first is to draw up a fuller genogram with Ruth, with ages and other information – fuller than was possible from the data with which I had supplied her for her own example of a genogram for Ruth's family. This Ruth did, and a conflation of her different diagrams in produced as Fig. 7.

Ruth also answered the various questions which Walrond-Skinner raises. As I have noted, she sees herself as a family healer, as well as the one seen to cope efficiently and can therefore be 'put upon'. She does not know of any other similar figure in the family. She does not feel like anyone else in the family, and therefore feels at odds with them all, and therefore she questions: 'Do I even belong to them?' The person to whom she feels closest is her mother, although there is also some resentment because Ruth thinks that her mother 'would like to lead her life through me'. She described how there was conflict with her mother, but that she was very close at one time, and that her mother is probably closest of all in the family to her now. Her father is distant and lives in a world of his own, and Ruth is distant from father. She shuns attempts on either of their parts to come close physically – 'I cringe'. She hated her brother in her early teens, when they 'fought like cat and dog', but in her later teens they got on very well. She moved out into service quarters at the end of her teens. But Ruth told me the story for the first time of not being invited to her brother's wedding, which was attended only by the parents on each side of the family.

Her father, she thinks, is closest to her brother. She feels that it is her relationship with her father which is the least satisfactory. This surprised me as the therapist, since I had been under the impression that of the two this was the parent to whom she was closest.

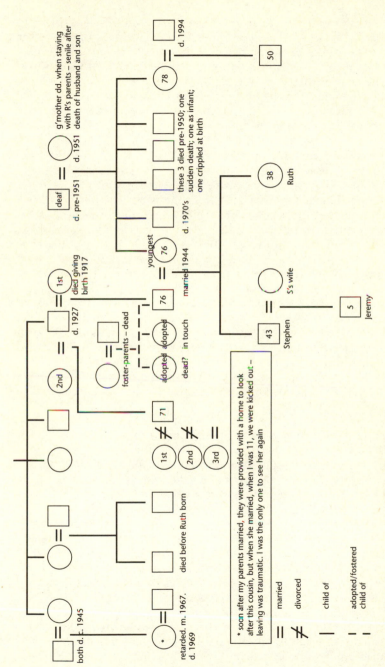

Figure 7 Ruth's extension of her genogram

In fact, the surprise was so great that I am sure that it is useful to clarify, with the type of questions which Walrond-Skinner suggests, the relationships in the family in such a comparative way. It is easy to build up a false impression from one or two highly charged events.

The change that Ruth would like to achieve in her relationship with her parents is to be more accepting of their inability to provide for her intimate needs, rather than actually shunning away any attempts: 'I might then be more accepting to cope with their trying and not fulfilling my total expectation'.

The second area in which Walrond-Skinner makes a definite proposal is in 'coaching' Ruth in tackling the least satisfactory relationship and in trying to create some change within it. Perhaps Walrond-Skinner took her lead from me when she imagined, as I had done, that the relationship which would need coaching is the one with mother. Indeed, this is the one which Ruth took and wrote about in her notes, although she may herself at that point have been taking the lead in turn from the supervisor's suggestion of working on the relationship with mother. Thus, if I have indeed had the wrong impression, the wrong impression now gets fed back to the client, through the supervisor, and with the power of the supervisor's word back into the therapy. How careful one must be! Ruth's response to Walrond-Skinner's set of questions had been that the relationship with her father was the least satisfactory, and although distant with both parents, 'probably dad more'.

Nevertheless, applying the coaching to the relationship with her mother, Ruth responded to the points which Walrond-Skinner makes. I quote Ruth's words:

From birth factually I am of the opinion that not much 'bonding' took place with mum. My mother struggled to breastfeed my older brother and decided she would not try with me. The birth was at home; the midwife picked me up by my feet (to weigh me!) and introduced my brother to me who went off screaming at my crying. I wanted cuddling as a child from mum (now I would like it from a partner).

I'm resentful that mum did not try with me. I'm not there in my own right is the feeling I have, which is compounded now when my brother's family comes to stay. This makes me angry. I would express it now by snide remarks rather than openness. It seem pointless to confront or be angry. Of course there is grief and loss of lack of closeness, with a real petulance of 'I want it from elsewhere' rather than from parents. It would be more satisfying too, and mature rather than child fantasies re-lived.

Ruth made some attempt to build some empathy between her own experiences and those of her mother. Her journey to Leicester with her was an occasion for this. She could see her mother's isolation after her marriage ('although not before it – afterwards she did have dad'). She was herself trying to break out of that mould. She also discovered in the weeks that followed working on Walrond-Skinner's material that by taking one of her parents out one at a time, rather than together, each was able to talk more with her. 'I think it has been positive, as well as hard work. It often leaves me with a sense of deprivation and energy loss'.

The last area of coaching had little specific content to it in Ruth's eyes. She remained cautious about talking about the event which clearly dominated her childhood – the rape by her brother's friends. Ruth thought that her parents did not know about it – they knew that her brother was interfering with her, and they told him off, although they said nothing at all to her about it. The rape, she thinks, was not mentioned by anyone, even by the neighbours who knew. What happened then was that sexual feelings clearly became a taboo subject, and she did not feel she could talk about them to her mother. I nevertheless had a sense that Ruth had seen some parallels between herself and her mother (although she did not believe her mother had also been abused), and had found some new understanding of her.

The third suggestion that Walrond-Skinner makes, that of inviting the family in for a session, was not one which appealed to Ruth for reasons I have already described above. She also commented upon Walrond-Skinner's concluding words that she 'will be unable to fully separate from my birth family until I have fully joined it'. Ruth wrote:

> I sense that 'good enough' emotional closeness may be
> through substitute parents who respond, or those who
> receive me for whom I am now. It is they who have helped
> me grow thus far. The church and Michael have given me
> more encouragement than a life-time with blood relations.
> My understanding does not aid acceptance or replenishment
> of what was lost.

Nevertheless, if at first Ruth questioned the idea that she need belong to the family in order to leave it, in a later session she could see just how much need there was for that, particularly as the older generation was ageing and would not be alive for many more years. She continued to experience 'incredible grief over these losses in the family, leaving me very isolated'. Yet remarkably she began to talk much more deeply with her brother Stephen about the family, and how he felt about the difficulty contacting other members of the wider family. She discovered that he felt like her, 'sad, restricted in making approaches, and unable to understand our parents' wish to remain isolated'. It felt as if their once close relationship (in her late teens) was being restored.

What Sue Walrond-Skinner could not know when she wrote her contribution to me, although she clearly sensed the issue, was that Ruth had already decided (in the last few weeks before reading this contribution) that she wanted to leave her parents' home and find a place of her own. Her experience in service accommodation in the past, including losing friends she had made outside the RAF, had perhaps partly held her back in the past. What held her back in the present was being largely unemployed, and therefore being unable to afford a mortgage. She was not sure what assistance her parents might give her, although she was aware that her brother had received help from them when he was in the position of seeking a place of his own. But she was actively looking for a property that would be closer to her own friends and to her church.

The extracts I quote here from what Ruth wrote, when she read through the suggestions which Sue Walrond-Skinner made, indicate the importance she attached to working through the assignments, and to the value of the tasks. Given the time she had already spent reflecting upon her life and her family history, there was little that was new in any of this, although, as Walrond-Skinner observes in her description of family therapy, those who see family history as a personal construction as much as a reality could reply that our view of our family's history is likely to change as therapy proceeds. A once-for-all history, taken at the beginning, is deceptive. My own sense was that in pulling it all together, and in giving it a tangible form – in genograms and in writing – this was helpful to Ruth, as well as to myself as the therapist.

Walrond-Skinner mentions the issue of touch, but she does not provide me with much help over it in her suggestions for practical tasks. What she more usefully picks up is the other question, which Conradi's questions to me also identified, of how long Ruth's therapy needs to go on. The issue of belonging to the family enough in order to be able to leave it may have its own parallel in Ruth being able to feel that she belongs enough to me in order to leave me. The concluding section of this chapter is written nearly two years after the session I took to my five supervisors; and that session was itself nearly two years after the start of Ruth's therapy. The critical (or impatient) reader might expect that Ruth has been able to move on during that time, and the signs are indeed there that her wish to move from home are another even more obvious expression of her wish to 'jump the gap' on the assault course which she talked about in the session. Sue Walrond-Skinner, in joining the project when she did, and talking her questions through with me some nine months after the other four, reflects (as I suspect I did when I spoke with her) the way the therapeutic focus had been shifting.

General comments

I have made detailed comments on each of the five supervisors, in which I have included the valuable responses which Ruth herself discussed in her sessions. Although most of the supervisors are supportive of my better responses and of some of my more helpful contributions to the therapy, thereby making it easier for me to look critically with them at those areas which are not going well, what I have missed in all of them is sufficient appreciation that the session recorded was an interaction between two people, in which my responses were evoked by Ruth's situation and manner, as much as (as they do indeed point out) her responses and feelings were at times evoked by me. It may be a false impression on my part, due to my own personality, but I felt rather more support and encouragement for what I was doing in the early stages of the three women's contributions than I did in the case of the two male supervisors. It was important for me to feel I may have done something right for me to be able to go on to look at where I was failing to see what my client was saying or what she needed from me.

I think none of the supervisors acknowledge sufficiently that I bring this to them as a hard session, one which makes me self-critical, and which therefore concerns me. This may be made more difficult for them by the nature of the exercise: it is largely a paper exercise, so that I cannot respond immediately, or even challenge an assumption made early on before it is then used as a thread followed throughout the supervision session. They may find it difficult to identify with me. Sue Walrond-Skinner understands the extent of the exposure on all our parts – Ruth's, mine and the supervisors – and this helped me feel a sense of cooperativeness. Melanie Fennell's description of the session as a 'golden moment in therapy' whetted my appetite to make more of its preciousness.

None of these supervisors know my work from other cases, as they would were I to be seeing any of them regularly, and this puts not only them but also me at a disadvantage. That might have been more fully acknowledged. For example, I too was concerned about the length of my responses which two or three of them observe, and knew that they were longer than usual (even longer in this session than usual with Ruth). Prue Conradi got the nearest to this area of concern in me when she asked me whether this was normal in my work. Even this did not prevent her from suggesting shorter responses, without looking at why my responses might have been longer than usual.

My awareness of Ruth's frailty and her need for comfort was high during that session, and I suspect that I came out of that session having imbued some of those feelings myself. I could have wished for a greater sense of my own frailty and of my need too for comfort in some of my supervisors. While acknowledging that I did not provide as much empathy as I could have done, I felt throughout my reading of the supervisors' contributions that I would have liked more sense of a supervisor who could identify with me in that session, and understand why I might have responded in the way I did; in other words, what was going on in the situation that might have led to it being the way it was. Searles makes the point well in his paper on supervision:

> One of my most oft-repeated experiences is that when I point out to the student how he should have responded, without helping him to discover what factors in the patient's psychopathology made it difficult for him to respond, I do not actually help him ... Typically ... he was responding ... to one aspect of the patient's ambivalence and was so absorbed in that as to be unaware of another aspect of that ambivalence which struck a particular chord in the supervisor.
>
> (Searles 1965: 589)

These are the sole negative comments I wish to make generally about the supervisory process that is described in this book. I am sure that there would not have been such obvious omissions had I been involved in face-to-face supervision, where my own non-verbal or more immediate verbal response would have shown my own needs as well as those of my client. I have heard of some supervisors who only concentrate on the client's material, and who appear to have no time for the counsellor's or the therapist's feelings; but I suspect this has been distorted here because of the atypical way in which this particular supervisory process has been conducted. Prue Conradi comes the closest to the more typical opportunity for the supervisee to work on his or her own feelings, and the way in which these interfere with or are provoked by the therapeutic process, as well as the supervision itself.

The one supervisor who insisted that he see me in face-to-face supervision looked with me at what bells the session rang for me, and what bells Ruth rang for me personally. Unfortunately, he was the one supervisor who failed to produce a written contribution. I remember how helpful I found it to recall how I might be feeling sorry for Ruth in the way I could feel sorry for someone in my own family of origin, and therefore how I might (in some sense against my better judgement) give her more by way of time and reduction of fee (and that one hug!) than I would normally consider beneficial. With that exception, which I can obviously only allude to here from my memory of the session, I am aware that while Ruth has revealed so much of her life in this book, my supervisors have not generally asked me to reveal much of me: they have confined themselves to my work, my style of therapy, and to my life as a professional, but not the person behind the therapist. These surely are factors which the supervisor needs to take into account as much as the therapist's own psychotherapist, even if it is debatable just how much of this personal material should be admitted into supervision.

I have not found it as troublesome as it might be for some other therapists to work with five supervisors of such different orientations. Indeed, it has provided evidence of the value of having different experiences of supervision, although not normally at the same time! Ruth herself has I think positively thrived upon the opportunities to try different methods, with her ability to enter into alternative ways of exploring issues making itself very evident to the reader. Perhaps that has made it easier for me to try these ideas out. I have found some of the exercises very helpful, suggested principally by Melanie Fennell and Sue Walrond-Skinner, although I have never lost sight of what other meanings I might want to look for in what appear to be straightforward answers to straightforward questions. I do not easily lose my immersion in psychodynamic thought and practice. I have enjoyed those busier sessions, but I have also yearned at times in them for a slower pace, and time to think, to reflect, to listen; and to adopt more of that empathic stance which Alan Cartwright and Prue Conradi have stressed, and to listen carefully to the coded messages which David Smith's contribution (if at times over-zealous in its application) has underlined, and which remains with me as an essential caution against all the illusions of the good that therapists are doing and against all the fantasies about the insight with which I think I am endowed.

If this is a book about supervision, it is also a book about Ruth, about a therapist, and about the work of five supervisors. It is also about a remarkable experience of therapy in which, unusually for most therapists, the work in supervision has for a time become part of the therapy itself. I believe that in itself (apart from the individual help given by the supervisors) this has also benefited Ruth, even though it has been a strange experience for her too. She has said that it has been positive and beneficial. The reader may want to know, on this final page, what has happened to her, and what point the therapy has reached. It takes a long time to produce a book (just as I remain of the view that it takes a long time for attitudes, behaviour and lives to change), and the process of publication which was started over two years ago, as I write, will not be complete for at least another six months. Ruth's therapy, which started (as I write) nearly four years ago, is not yet over. I cannot predict (although I do not have the same anxiety about it that at one point I did) when it will finish, although she has hinted that it will be about the time this book is published. I think, judging by Ruth's response to the work involved in this book, that it will never be over, because although her therapy with me will finish, both she and I will carry on the process of understanding it and ourselves for many years to come.

References

Casement, P. (1985). *On Learning from the Patient*. London: Tavistock/ Routledge.

Ferenczi, S. (1955). *Final Contributions to the Problems and Methods of Psycho-analysis*. London: Hogarth Press.

Jacobs, M. (1996). Parallel process: confirmation and critique. *Journal of Psychodynamic Counselling*, Vol. 2, 1, pp. 55–66.

Jones, R. (1989). Supervision: a choice between equals? *British Journal of Psychotherapy*, Vol. 5, pp. 505–511.

Searles, H. (1965). Problems of psycho-analytic supervision. In *Collected Papers on Schizophrenia and Related Subjects*. London: Hogarth Press.

Winnicott, D.W. (1975). *Collected Papers: Through Paediatrics to Psycho-analysis*. London: Tavistock.

MORAG – MYSELF OR MOTHER HEN?

Moira Walker (ed.)

'I don't like cleaning and hoovering and washing up. I do them because I have to, and I feel that James wants me to be in the house, to be there because his children are there, and the family's there . . . he likes me there being the mother-hen!'

This is how Morag begins to tell her story to her potential therapist. Six therapists are given the opportunity of assessing Morag: What do they wish to know about her? How might they work with her? And what outcome can they predict for her as a result of therapy?

In this highly original book – which starts with Morag's own story – the reader has a chance to see six different therapists at work, drawing on the same material from the one real client. The similarities and differences between therapies are highlighted. And at the end the reader is able to enter Morag's experience of the process, and decide with her, which one she might choose in her search for a therapist.

This fascinating volume will appeal to a wide range of students and practitioners involved in counselling and psychotherapy, particularly those interested in comparing different therapeutic approaches.

Contents
The editors: in search of the client – Morag: myself or mother hen? – The reader's response – Roxanne Agnew: focused expressive psychotherapy – Windy Dryden: rational emotive behaviour therapy – Paul Holmes: psychodrama – Arthur Jonathan: existential psychotherapy – Anthea Millar: Adlerian therapy – Peter Savage: hypnotherapy – Moira Walker and Morag: review and response.

Contributors
Roxanne Agnew, Windy Dryden, Paul Holmes, Athur Jonathan, Anthea Millar, Peter Savage.

176pp   0 335 19224 6 (Paperback)

PETA – A FEMINIST'S PROBLEM WITH MEN

Moira Walker (ed.)

'I've got a problem with men . . . I don't know whether it's a problem with other things as well . . . I am afraid of what men represent . . . I feel they have more power.'

This is how Peta begins to tell her story to her potential therapist. Six therapists are given the opportunity of assessing Peta: What do they wish to know about her? How do they understand her? How might they work with her? And what outcome can they predict for her as a result of therapy?

In this fascinating book – which starts with Peta's own story – the reader has the chance to see six different therapists at work, drawing on the same initial material from the one real client. The similarities and differences between therapies and therapists are highlighted. And at the end the reader is able to enter Peta's experience of the process, and decide with her, which one she might choose in her search for a therapist.

This highly original volume will appeal to a wide range of students and practitioners involved in counselling and psychotherapy, particularly those interested in comparing different therapeutic approaches.

Contents
The editors: in search of the client – Peta: a feminist's problem with men – The reader's response – Jennifer Mackewn: Gestalt psychotherapy – Judy Moore: person-centred psychotherapy – John Ormrod: cognitive behaviour therapy – John Rowan: humanistic and integrative psychotherapy – Maye Taylor: feminist psychotherapy – Christine Wood: art therapy – Moira Walker and Peta: review and response.

Contributors
Jennifer Mackewn, Judy Moore, John Ormrod, John Rowan, Maye Taylor, Christine Wood.

168pp   0 335 19223 8 (paperback)

CHARLIE – AN UNWANTED CHILD?

Michael Jacobs (ed.)

'All the while I very much got the impression when I was young that my mother didn't love me and doesn't love me. I think of myself as unlovable . . .'

These are Charlie's opening words to her potential therapist. Six therapists are given the opportunity of assessing Charlie: What do they wish to know about her? How do they understand her? How might they work with her? And what outcome can they predict for her as a result of therapy?

In this fascinating book – which starts with Charlie's own story – the reader has the chance to see six different therapists at work, drawing on the same initial material from the one real client. The similarities and differences between therapies and therapists are highlighted. And at the end the reader is able to enter Charlie's experience of the process, and decide with her, which one she might choose in her search for a therapist.

This highly original volume will appeal to a wide range of students and practitioners involved in counselling and psychotherapy, particularly those interested in comparing different therapeutic approaches.

Contents
The editors: in search of the client – Charlie: an unwanted child? – The reader's response – Cassie Cooper: Kleinian psychotherapy – Phil Lapworth: transactional analysis – Frank Margison: psychoanalytic psychotherapy – Alix Pirani: humanistic-transpersonal psychotherapy – Anthony Ryle: cognitive-analytic therapy – Claire Wintram: feminist group therapy – Michael Jacobs and Charlie: review and response.

Contributors
Cassie Cooper, Phil Lapworth, Frank Margison, Alix Pirani, Anthony Ryle, Claire Wintram.

176pp   0 335 19199 1 (paperback)